At Issue

I Alternatives to Prisons

Other Books in the At Issue Series:

At Issue

|Alternatives to Prisons

Ronald D. Lankford, Jr., Book Editor

GREENHAVEN PRESS
A part of Gale, Cengage Learning

GALE
CENGAGE Learning·

Detroit • New York • San Francisco • New Haven, Conn • Waterville, Maine • London

Elizabeth Des Chenes, *Managing Editor*

© 2012 Greenhaven Press, a part of Gale, Cengage Learning.

Gale and Greenhaven Press are registered trademarks used herein under license.

For more information, contact:
Greenhaven Press
27500 Drake Rd.
Farmington Hills, MI 48331-3535
Or you can visit our Internet site at gale.cengage.com

For product information and technology assistance, contact us at

Gale Customer Support, 1-800-877-4253
For permission to use material from this text or product, submit all requests online at www.cengage.com/permissions.

Further permissions questions can be e-mailed to permissionrequest@cengage.com.

Articles in Greenhaven Press anthologies are often edited for length to meet page require-ments. In addition, original titles of these works are changed to clearly present the main thesis and to explicitly indicate the author's opinion. Every effort is made to ensure that Greenhaven Press accurately reflects the original intent of the authors. Every effort has been made to trace the owners of copyrighted material.

Cover image copyright © Illumination Works.

LIBRARY OF CONGRESS CATALOGING-IN-PUBLICATION DATA

Alternatives to prisons / Ronald D. Lankford, Jr., book editor.
    p. cm. -- (At issue)
    Includes bibliographical references and index.
    ISBN 978-0-7377-5544-2 (hbk.) -- ISBN 978-0-7377-5545-9 (pbk.)
    1. Alternatives to imprisonment--United States. 2. Corrections--United States. 3. Criminals--Rehabilitation--United States. 4. Criminal justice, Administration of--United States. I. Lankford, Ronald D., 1962-
    HV9304.A6473 2011
    364.6'8--dc23
                                                                    2011034694

Printed in the United States of America
2 3 4 5 6 7 15 14 13 12

Contents

Introduction

Through the 1980s, conservatives and liberals seemed to line up on opposite sides of the prison debate. As prison populations continued to grow, conservatives remained tough on crime, advocating new prison construction, while liberals argued that prisons only served to further educate detainees in a life of crime. During the 1990s and beyond, the dividing line began to move. During the last several years, liberals and conservatives have often found themselves on the same side of the prison issue. While many reasons have been cited for this change, one has stood out: state funding.

As prison populations grew to record numbers in the 2000s, states found it increasingly difficult to fund incarceration. In a number of states, more money was being spent on prisons than on public education. In 2010, the Pew Center on the States noted, "State corrections spending, driven almost entirely by prison expenditures, has quadrupled over the past two decades, making it the second fastest growing area of state budgets, trailing only Medicaid. Total state spending on corrections today is more than $50 billion a year."[1] The financial burden of prisons became even clearer following the recession in 2008 and beyond. Simply put, many states could no longer afford their prison system.

The High Cost of Prison

In 2011, the Pew Center on the States reported that nearly half of the inmates released from prison would return within three years.[2] This study underlined the need for new solutions: whatever the reason for recidivism (return to prison), prison populations would continue to increase; as they con-

1. "Pew Finds That One in Ten Prisoners Return to Prison within Three Years," Pew Charitable Trusts, press release, April 12, 2011. www.pewtrusts.org.
2. Pew Center on the States, *State of Recidivism: The Revolving Door of America's Prisons*, Public Safety Performance Project, April 2011. www.pewcenteronthestates.org.

tinued to grow, the cost of maintaining prisons would also continue to increase. Confirming this, the cost of prison for the states rose from $63 billion in 1997 to $74 billion in 2007; local government spending on prisons also increased from $99 billion to $116 billion between 1997 and 2007. Currently, the average cost of housing and feeding a prisoner in the United States is approximately $28,000 per year.

In California, for instance, prison costs helped create record budget shortfalls in 2010–11. The average cost of incarceration in California is approximately $44,000 per year. Overcrowding added to the state's prison problem: California's prison system is currently operating at 160 percent of capacity. Similar problems have plagued other states. In South Carolina, the prison population has exploded during the last 25 years, requiring $394 million dollars per year to maintain. The total cost of the South Carolina prison system is estimated to reach $458 million per year in 2014.

With crowding, increased costs, and shrinking state budgets, lawmakers understood that drastic changes needed to be enacted. "Policies aimed at reducing recidivism offer perhaps the ripest opportunities for achieving the twin goals of less crime and lower costs," said Adam Gelb of the Pew Center. "State leaders from across the political spectrum are finding they can agree on strategies that do a better job of turning offenders from tax burdens into taxpayers."[3] Many of these solutions focused on prison reform and alternative sentencing.

Prison Reform and Savings

One thing that simplified the issue of prison reform was that many legislators found it easy to agree on which prisoners should be considered for alternative sentencing: non-violent offenders. During the 1980s, for instance, the criminal justice

---

3. "Pew Finds That One in Ten Prisoners Return to Prison within Three Years," *Pew Charitable Trusts*, press release, April 12, 2011. www.pewtrusts.org.

system began to incarcerate more people for minor drug offenses not involving violent episodes. By 1997, a million of the 1.8 million detainees in American prisons were considered nonviolent. While few politicians were willing to advocate for the legalization of drugs or other crimes, many suggested that alternative sentences such as parole and drug rehabilitation might be more effective and less costly than traditional prison.

One notable transformation has taken place in Texas, a state that gained a reputation as tough on crime along with being the most frequent enacter of the death penalty during the 1990s. "Texas has turned a few heads in recent years by becoming a leader in community corrections and alternatives to incarceration," wrote Matt Kelly at Change.Org.[4] Adding a number of alternatives, from drug courts to probation, Texas' prison population decreased by 1,257 detainees between 2008 and 2009.

One of the more innovative programs in Texas involves placing criminals in a reading program, Changing Lives Through Literature. Within the program, participants read and discuss classic books. "Repeat offenders of serious crimes such as armed robbery, assault or drug dealing are made to attend a reading group where they discuss literary classics such as *To Kill a Mockingbird, The Bell Jar,* and *Of Mice and Men*," noted Anna Barker in the *Guardian*.[5] While the program may only impact a small number of persons within the criminal justice system, its very existence revealed how much the justice community had changed since the 1990s.

Prison Abolition

While alternatives to prison have become more commonplace, it remains unclear how far prison reform will go. Commentators have suggested the possibility of "prisons without walls," a

4. Matt Kelly, "It's Time for Texas to Close Some Prisons," Change.Org, December 28, 2010. http://news.change.org.
5. Anna Barker, "Novel Approach: Reading Courses as an Alternative to Prison," *Guardian*, July 21, 2010. www.guardian.co.uk.

vision that would allow most criminals to remain outside of prison while wearing tracking devices. Other groups have called for the abolition of prisons, arguing that incarceration in America violates basic human rights. Even as states shut down costly prisons and choose alternatives, however, there seems to be little political momentum to completely dismantle the incarceration system in America. While traditional prison may be an expensive option, it remains a popular one for violent criminals.

Even while embracing alternatives to prison, one problem remains: at present there seems to be little information on the success of individual programs. While officials endorse alternatives to prison, then, there are few surveys detailing which programs work and which do not. Even with programs that are considered successful like drug courts, critics argue that the results have been stacked. If only low-level offenders are admitted to the program, for instance, then a higher success rate is guaranteed. Even without hard data, prison alternatives seem likely to remain an attractive option as governments at all levels continue to aim for balanced budgets.

1

The American Prison System Is Ineffective and Requires Reform

Jennifer Gonnerman

Jennifer Gonnerman is a contributing writer to Mother Jones *and the author of the National Book Award finalist* Life on the Outside.

America has the highest incarceration rate in the world. America's addiction to the penal system is both expensive and destructive to individual lives. Many of the punishments within the system, such as decades spent in solitary confinement, are irrational and border on inhumane. Worse still, America's prisons rarely reform prisoners: many, once released, will re-enter a correctional facility. America needs to find alternatives to the current system, offering true rehabilitation and a proper education for prisoners. Otherwise, there is a danger of creating a divided society in which millions of former prisoners no longer have their full rights as citizens.

The number first appeared in headlines earlier this year: Nearly one in four of all prisoners worldwide is incarcerated in America. It was just the latest such statistic. Today, one in nine African American men between the ages of 20 and 34 is locked up. In 1970, our prisons held fewer than 200,000 people; now that number exceeds 1.5 million, and when you add in local jails, it's 2.3 million—1 in 100 American adults.

Since the 1980s, we've sat by as the numbers inched higher and our prison system ballooned, swallowing up an ever-larger portion of the citizenry. But do statistics like these, no matter how disturbing, really mean anything anymore? What does it take to get us to sit up and notice?

Apparently, it takes a looming financial crisis. For there is another round of bad news, the logical extension of the first: The more money a state spends on building and running prisons, the less there is for everything else, from roads and bridges to health care and public schools. At the pace our inmate population has been expanding, America's prison system is becoming, quite simply, too expensive to sustain. That is why Kansas, Texas, and at least 11 other states have been trying out new strategies to curb the cost—reevaluating their parole policies, for instance, so that not every parolee who runs afoul of an administrative rule is shipped straight back to prison. And yet our infatuation with incarceration continues.

There are many people behind bars who you would not want as your neighbor, but in our hunger for justice we have lost perspective.

Number One in Incarceration

There have been numerous academic studies and policy reports and journalistic accounts analyzing our prison boom, but this phenomenon cannot be fully measured in numbers. That much became apparent to me when, beginning in 2000, I spent nearly four years shadowing a woman who'd just been released from prison. She'd been locked up for 16 years for a first-time drug crime, and her absence had all but destroyed her family. Her mother had taken in her four young children after her arrest, only to die prematurely of kidney failure. One daughter was deeply depressed, the other was seething with rage, and her youngest son had followed her lead, diving into the neighborhood drug culture and then winding up in prison himself.

The criminal justice system had punished not only her but her entire family. How do you measure the years of wasted hours—riding on a bus to a faraway prison, lining up to be scanned and searched and questioned, sitting in a bleak visiting room waiting for a loved one to walk in? How do you account for all the dollars spent on collect calls from prison—calls that can cost at least three times as much as on the outside because the prison system is taking a cut? How do you begin to calculate the lessons absorbed by children about deprivation and punishment and vengeance? How do you end the legacy of incarceration?

America is expert at turning citizens into convicts, but we've forgotten how to transform convicts back into citizens.

This is not to say that nobody deserves to go to prison or that we should release everyone who is now locked up. There are many people behind bars who you would not want as your neighbor, but in our hunger for justice we have lost perspective. We treat 10-year sentences like they're nothing, like that's a soft penalty, when in much of the rest of the world a decade behind bars would be considered extraordinarily severe. This is what separates us from other industrialized countries: It's not just that we send so many people to prison, but that we keep them there for so long and send them back so often. Eight years ago, we surpassed Russia to claim the dubious distinction of having the world's highest rate of incarceration; today we're still No. 1.

If awards were granted to the country with the most surreal punishments, we would certainly win more than our share. Thirty-six straight years in solitary confinement (the fate of two men convicted in connection with the murder of a guard in Louisiana's Angola prison). A 55-year sentence for a small-time pot dealer who carried a gun during his sales (handed down by a federal court in Utah in 2004). Life sentences for 13-year-olds. (In 2005, Human Rights Watch counted more than 2,000 American inmates serving life without parole for crimes committed as juveniles. The entire rest of the world has only locked up 12 kids without hope of release.) Female prisoners forced to wear shackles while giving birth. (Amnesty International found 48 states that permitted this practice as of 2006.) A ban on former prisoners working as barbers (on the books in New York state).

Creating Second-Class Citizens

America is expert at turning citizens into convicts, but we've forgotten how to transform convicts back into citizens. In 1994, Congress eliminated Pell grants for prisoners, a move that effectively abolished virtually all of the 350 prison college programs across the country. That might not seem like a catastrophe, until you consider that education has been *proven* to help reduce recidivism. (This was the conclusion of a recent paper by the Urban Institute, which reviewed 49 separate studies.) As the *New York Times*' Adam Liptak has pointed out, our prisons used to be models of redemption; de Tocqueville praised them in *Democracy in America*. Many prisons still call themselves "correctional facilities," but the term has become a misnomer. Most abandoned any pretense of rehabilitation long ago. Former California governor Jerry Brown even went so far as to rewrite the state's penal code to stress that the primary mission of that state's prisons is punishment.

Our cell blocks are packed with men and women who cannot read or write, who never graduated from high school—75 percent of state inmates—who will be hardpressed to find a job once they are released. Once freed, they become second-class citizens. Depending on the state, they may be denied public housing, student loans, a driver's license, welfare benefits, and a wide range of jobs. Perhaps there is no more damning statistic than the fact that within three years, half will be convicted of a new crime.

We've become a two-tier society in which millions of ostensibly free people are prohibited from enjoying the rights and privileges accorded to everyone else.

Recently, there have been some hopeful signs. In April, the Second Chance Act was finally signed into law; it will provide federal grants to programs that help prisoners reenter society. But our punishment industry—which each year spends millions lobbying federal and state lawmakers—has grown so massive and so entrenched that it will take far more than one piece of legislation to begin to undo its far-reaching effects.

Just look at our felony disenfranchisement laws, which prohibit 5.3 million people from voting—including 13 percent of African American men. These numbers actually underestimate the scope of the problem, as many ex-prisoners believe they cannot vote even if they can. And so the legacy of our prison boom continues: We've become a two-tier society in which millions of ostensibly free people are prohibited from enjoying the rights and privileges accorded to everyone else— and we continue to be defined by our desire for punishment and revenge, rather than by our belief in the power of redemption.

2

There Are Many Alternatives to Incarceration

Families Against Mandatory Minimums

Families Against Mandatory Minimums is the national voice for fair and proportionate sentencing laws, working to mobilize thousands of individuals and families whose lives are adversely affected by unjust sentences.

While prison has often been used as a punishment for criminals in America, there are many alternatives that are less expensive and more effective at reducing crime. Drug courts, for instance, allow individuals convicted of drug-related crimes an alternative to prison. Under the supervision of the court and with the help of drug counseling, individuals can continue to work and live with their families. There are many other programs including probation, halfway houses, home confinement, fines, and community service that also offer effective alternatives. Mental health courts work in a similar manner to drug courts, while public shaming for crimes like drunk driving help discourage illegal behavior. Alternative sentencing offers a wide variety of choices, allowing courts to match the special sentence to the individual.

An "alternative to incarceration" is any kind of punishment other than time in prison or jail that can be given to a person who commits a crime.

Frequently, punishments other than prison or jail time place serious demands on offenders and provide them with

Families Against Mandatory Minimums, "Alternatives to Incarceration Fact Sheet," FAMM.org, July 30, 2009. Copyright © 2009 by Families Against Mandatory Minimums (FAMM). All rights reserved. Reproduced by permission.

intensive court and community supervision. Just because a certain punishment does not involve time in prison or jail does not mean it is "soft on crime" or a "slap on the wrist." Alternatives to incarceration can repair harms suffered by victims, provide benefits to the community, treat the drug-addicted or mentally ill, and rehabilitate offenders. Alternatives can also reduce prison and jail costs and prevent additional crimes in the future. Before we can maximize the benefits of alternatives to incarceration, however, we must repeal mandatory minimums and give courts the power to use cost-effective, recidivism-reducing sentencing options instead.

FAMM supports the creation and use of alternatives to incarceration because:

- *They give courts more sentencing options.* Each offender and crime is unique, and prison or jail time may not always be the most effective response. If courts have options other than incarceration, they can better tailor a cost-effective sentence that fits the offender and the crime, protects the public, and provides rehabilitation.

- *They save taxpayers money.* It costs almost $28,000 to keep one person in federal prison for one year (some states' prison costs are much higher). Alternatives to incarceration are cheaper, help prevent prison and jail overcrowding, and save taxpayers millions.

- *They strengthen families and communities.* Prison or jail time separates the offender from his or her spouse and children, sometimes for decades at a time. Alternatives to incarceration keep people with their families, in their neighborhoods and jobs, and allow them to earn money, pay taxes, and contribute to their communities.

- *They protect the public by reducing crime.* Over 40 percent of all people leaving prison will reoffend and be back in prison within three years of their release. Alternatives to prison such as drug and mental health courts are proven to confront the underlying causes of crime (i.e., drug addiction and mental illness) and help prevent offenders from committing new crimes.

- *The public supports alternatives to incarceration.* Eight in ten (77 percent) adults believe that alternatives to incarceration (probation, restitution, community service, and/or rehabilitative services) are the most appropriate sentence for nonviolent, non-serious offenders and that prison or jail are appropriate only if these alternatives fail.

[Drug court program components] give the court authority to praise and reward the offender for successes and discipline the offender for failures.

Some of the most frequently used alternatives to incarceration are described on the following pages. More alternatives exist, but are too numerous to be included here.

Drug Courts—Drug courts are a special branch of courts created within already-existing court systems. Drug courts provide court-supervised drug treatment and community supervision to offenders with substance abuse problems. All 50 states and the District of Columbia have at least a few drug court programs. There are no drug courts in the federal system. Some states have drug courts for adults and for juveniles, as well as family treatment or family dependency treatment courts that treat parents so that they might remain or reunite with their children. Drug court eligibility requirements and program components vary from one locality to another, but they typically

- Require offenders to complete random urine tests, attend drug treatment counseling or Narcotics Anonymous/Alcoholics Anonymous meetings, meet with a probation officer, and report to the court regularly on their progress;

- Give the court authority to praise and reward the offender for successes and discipline the offender for failures (including sending the offender to jail or prison);

- Are available to nonviolent, substance-abusing offenders who meet specific eligibility requirements (e.g., no history of violence, few or no prior convictions);

- Are not available on demand—usually, either the prosecutor or the judge handling the case must refer the offender to drug court; sometimes, this referral can only be made after the offender pleads guilty to the offense; and

- Allow offenders who successfully complete the program to avoid pleading guilty, having a conviction placed on their record, or serving some or all of their prison or jail time; some programs also allow successful participants who have already pled guilty to have their drug conviction removed from their record.

Average cost: Between $1,500 and $11,000 per participant per year

Probation/Community Corrections—Usually referred to as "community corrections" in the states (however, the federal Bureau of Prisons uses the term "community corrections" to refer to halfway houses (see below), a different alternative to incarceration), probation keeps the offender in the community but puts limits and obligations on his freedom. Probation can come with many conditions attached, including meeting regularly with a probation officer, staying under house arrest during certain parts of the day, taking random urine tests, remaining drug-free, working, doing community service, and participating in substance abuse or mental health treatment. If an offender does not comply with the probation conditions, more stringent supervision can be required, or, if the violation is serious, probation can be revoked and the person can be required to serve time in jail or prison. There are different varieties of probation:

- On *Intensive Supervisory Probation and Parole (ISP)*, probation officers have fewer cases, monitor offenders more closely, and meet with offenders more often.

- *Day reporting* requires offenders to report to a location similar to a probation office on a daily basis. Here, they undergo daily drug and alcohol tests and inform their supervisors of their plans for the day, including where they will work or search for employment.

Average cost: Probation: $9.92 per day per participant (state average) $10.79 per day per participant (federal)

ISP: $6,000 per participant per year

Day Reporting: $20 per day per participant

Halfway houses may be a good choice when a person has served time in prison, been released on parole, and then violated a parole condition.

Halfway Houses—Halfway houses (also called "community correction centers" or "residential reentry centers" by the federal Bureau of Prisons) are used mostly as an intermediate housing option to help a person return from prison to the community after he has served a prison sentence. Sometimes, though, halfway houses can be used instead of prison or jail, usually when a person's sentence is very short. For example, halfway houses may be a good choice when a person has served time in prison, been released on parole, and then violated a parole condition and been ordered to serve a few months additional time for that violation. While in halfway houses, offenders are monitored and must fulfill conditions placed on them by the court. Usually, offenders must remain inside the halfway house except when they are going to court or to a job.

Average cost: $58–112 per day per participant (federal system)

Requiring the offender to pay supervision fees, fines, and court costs can be used as an independent punishment or in addition to other punishments.

Home Confinement/Electronic Home Monitoring—Home confinement (also called "house arrest") requires offenders to stay in their homes except when they are in certain pre-approved areas (i.e., at court or work). Often, home confinement requires that the offender be placed on electronic home monitoring (EHM). EHM requires offenders to wear an electronic device, such as an ankle bracelet, that sends a signal to a transmitter and lets the authorities know where the offender is at all times. Like probation, home confinement usually comes with conditions. If the offender violates those conditions, he can be put in jail or prison. Offenders on EHM usually contact a probation officer daily and take frequent and random drug tests. In many jurisdictions, an offender cannot be placed on EHM unless the court or a jail official recommends it.

Average cost: $5–15 per day per participant

Fines and Restitution—Requiring the offender to pay supervision fees, fines, and court costs can be used as an independent punishment or in addition to other punishments. "Tariff fines" are a set amount applied to every offender when a particular crime is committed (e.g., $500 for driving while intoxicated), regardless of the offender's income level or ability to pay. For the wealthy, tariff fines can be too small to be a meaningful punishment. For the poor, tariff fines can be too large, resulting in jail time when the offender cannot pay. "Day fines" are one solution. They are not a flat amount, but are based on the seriousness of the crime and the offender's daily income. Wealthier offenders pay more and pay an amount that is a meaningful loss of income, while those with lower incomes pay an amount they can afford and avoid jail. Restitution requires offenders to pay for some or all of a community or victim's medical costs or property loss that resulted from the crime.

Community Service—Community service can be its own punishment or can act as a condition of probation or an alternative to paying restitution or a fine (each hour of service reduces the fine or restitution by a particular amount, until it is paid in full). Community service is unpaid work by an offender for a civic or nonprofit organization. In federal courts, community service is not a sentence, but a special condition of probation or supervised release.

Restorative justice is holistic sentencing process focused on repairing harm and bringing healing to all those who are impacted by a crime, including the offender.

Sex Offender Treatment and Civil Commitment—Many sex offenders are placed on probation, with requirements that they attend a sex offender treatment program, report regularly to a probation officer, do not contact their victims, do not use the internet, and do not live or work in certain areas. Sex offender treatment programs can be inpatient (residential) or outpatient (non-residential) and generally use cognitive-behavioral therapy, counseling, and other approaches to reduce the likelihood that the person will commit another sex offense. About 20 states also have "civil commitment" programs, which place sex offenders in secure hospitals or residential treatment facilities for treatment. These offenders typically receive civil commitment only *after* they have finished serving a prison term for their sex offense. Offenders can be required to stay on civil commitment indefinitely, which means the programs can cost up to four times what it costs to keep an offender in prison.

Mental Health Courts—Mental health courts, like drug courts, are specialized courts that place offenders suffering from mental illness, mental disabilities, drug dependency, or serious personality disorders in a court-supervised, community-based mental health treatment program. Court and community supervision is combined with inpatient or outpatient professional mental health treatment. Offenders receive rewards for compliance with supervision conditions and are disciplined for noncompliance. They are also linked to housing, health care, and life skills training resources that help prevent relapse and promote their recovery. Often, offenders must first plead guilty to charges before being diverted to mental health court.

Restorative Justice—Restorative justice is a holistic sentencing process focused on repairing harm and bringing healing to all those who are impacted by a crime, including the offender. Representatives of the justice system, victims, offenders, and community members are involved and achieve these goals through sentencing circles, victim restitution, victim-offender mediation, and formalized community service programs. Sentencing circles occur when the victim, offender, community members, and criminal justice officials meet and jointly agree on a sentence that repairs the harm the offender caused. Victim-offender mediation allows the offender and victim to meet and exchange apologies and forgiveness for the crime committed. Restorative justice practices can be used alone or as a condition of a sentence of probation.

Boot Camp—Boot camp programs involve intense daily regimens that include physical exercise, individual counseling, educational classes, and studying for a GED. Today, boot camps are no longer used in the federal prison system and are rarely used in state corrections systems. Similar to a military boot camp, offenders follow a strict disciplinary code that requires them to wear short hair and uniforms, stand at attention before their officers, and address their superiors as "sir." Offenders who complete the program and find a job can become eligible for early release. Once released, they may be put on probation.

Public Shaming—Public shaming is public humiliation. It is used rarely and usually only for low-level misdemeanors. For example, a court ordered a convicted mail thief to stand outside a post office for a total of 100 hours wearing a sign that said, "I am a mail thief. This is my punishment." Public shaming is intended to rehabilitate the offender and discourage him from reoffending.

3

Community Corrections Provide Effective Alternatives to Prison

Joan Petersilia, as told to the Pew Center on the States

Joan Petersilia is a professor of criminology, law, and society at the University of California, Irvine. The Pew Center on the States is a division of the Pew Charitable Trusts that identifies and advances effective solutions to critical issues facing states.

The phrase "community corrections" is similar to "prison alternatives": community corrections focuses on nonprison solutions for individuals convicted of crimes. The two central goals of community corrections are to rehabilitate individuals and to save money. While there is very little information on which community corrections programs work the best, certain programs— house arrest and boot camps, for instance—may not work well. The most effective programs institute strategies that match the right individual to the right program. For anyone with a substance abuse problem, for instance, drug and alcohol testing is essential. Effective programs also work to reintegrate individuals into their communities. Prisons are still needed, but they should not be the first choice for the justice system.

[P ew:] *To start us off, what are community corrections and what are their goals?*

[Joan Petersilia:] Simply defined, "community corrections" are non-prison sanctions that are imposed on convicted adults or adjudicated juveniles either by a court instead of a prison sentence or by a parole board following release from prison. Community corrections programs are usually operated by probation and parole agencies, and the programs can include general community supervision as well as day reporting centers, halfway houses and other residential facilities, work release, and other community programs. All community corrections programs have the multiple goals of providing offender accountability, delivering rehabilitation services and surveillance, and achieving fiscal efficiency.

Would you describe a few of the most effective community corrections programs and the results they deliver?

First, it is important to note that probably 99 percent of all community corrections programs in the U.S. today have not been scientifically evaluated. So, identifying which ones are *most* effective is impossible. I suspect there are many excellent programs operating today (such as faith-based mentoring, etc.), which if subject to evaluation, might be effective. But the corrections literature includes evaluations mostly of large federally-funded programs, and most of those are services for drug-addicted felons. From that literature, we know that intensive community supervision combined with rehabilitation services can reduce recidivism between 10 and 20 percent. Some drug courts have also had similarly encouraging results.

And what does the research say about ineffective programs?

We know more about what doesn't work than what does. Research has shown that boot camps, house arrest, and routine probation and parole supervision do not reduce recidivism. But again, the majority of community corrections programs have never been scientifically tested so you have to view these results cautiously as well.

In your view, what are the principles or themes that run through effective community corrections programs?

At the core of any good community corrections program is the use of an objective risk and needs assessment. Assessments allow correctional agencies to assign offenders to the programs that will most likely benefit them. The "risk" part of the assessment instrument assesses risk to reoffend, and that information is critical to assigning probationers or parolees to levels of surveillance and supervision, such as specialized caseloads, frequent drug testing or electronic monitoring. The "need" portion of the assessment instrument identifies the subset of the offender population that research has shown will benefit from being in rehabilitation treatment programs. Research has shown that for high and moderate risk offenders, participation in treatment programs and services has high payoff, but for those with a low risk to reoffend, life skills programs are more appropriate. This is the most efficient use of scarce correctional resources as well as the best way to increase public safety.

Effective programs involve family and community members in a very real and proactive way.

Of course, the next core principle is to make certain that the rehabilitation programs are of sufficient quality to make a difference. There are now several scoring methods that rate the quality of rehabilitation programs along such dimensions as staff qualifications and training, use of a tested curriculum or program model, and use of cognitive-behavioral or social learning methods. These and other program characteristics have been shown to increase success. In short, effective corrections programs must get the right offender in the right program. And then of course, we must continually evaluate costs and program outcomes and revise accordingly.

Research over the last several decades also reinforces the importance of the community and familial supports as sources of informal social control. Effective programs involve family and community members in a very real and proactive way. Effective programs recognize that government programs ultimately end, and the hand-off between the formal and informal systems is ultimately what determines success. In my opinion, community corrections agencies that collaborate closely with non-profits and other community organizations, who in turn work to integrate the offender's family and social support system, will have the most success.

Sending someone to prison should be our last resort—it is expensive, it is stigmatizing, and it can increase risk for future criminal behavior.

How have community corrections programs changed and what does the future hold?

There are two major trends that I see in community corrections today. The first has to do with technology to monitor compliance with court-ordered conditions, such as drug testing, global positioning systems, alcohol breathalyzers, and so on. The second has to do with "wrap-around services." Every agency, including probation and parole, recognizes that reducing criminal behavior is incredibly difficult and no one agency can do it alone. More and more, I see wrap-around services, where mental health, alcohol and drug abuse, housing, and medical services agencies are planning an offender's case management plan together. This is very promising. And then, of course, there is reentry, which is now the new correctional buzzword. If inmate reentry were our focus, then the divide between incarceration and community corrections would begin to blur, and that would be a good thing, in my view.

Saving the best for last, what are the key questions policy makers should be asking when they confront decisions about correctional strategy and spending? How should they think about striking the right balance between building more prisons and expanding community corrections?

To me, policymakers need to understand that it is not one or the other: build prisons or support community corrections. We need strong systems of each. We need to create enough prison space to house the truly violent and those with no desire to change their criminal behavior and, at the same time, we need to invest heavily in helping offenders who are not yet steeped in criminal behavior and wish to chart a different path. Sending someone to prison should be our last resort—it is expensive, it is stigmatizing, and it can increase risk for future criminal behavior. Moreover, it impacts not only the person incarcerated but also his or her family and children. Investing in quality community corrections programs is, in my view, just good public policy.

4

Drug Courts Are Effective in Reducing Recidivism

Jessica Huseman

Jessica Huseman is an intern with the National Center for Policy Analysis.

Drug courts are a fairly recent addition to the criminal justice system. In 1988, there were no drug courts; in 2010, there were over 2,000 drug courts on the state level (there are no federal drug courts). Drug courts offer a prison alternative to convicted criminals who qualify; instead of going to prison, individuals receive treatment for addiction and are supervised by the court. Drug courts have been much more effective at reducing recidivism (returning to prison) than traditional prison sentences. Drug courts are also much less expensive than prisons. Unfortunately, drug courts only serve a small percentage of the individuals within the criminal justice system who would qualify for an alternative sentence. Expanding the current drug court system would offer a cost effective way to rehabilitate more convicted individuals.

Drug courts are judicially supervised programs that provide long-term treatment and other services to nonviolent drug law offenders. Cases can be referred to drug courts in lieu of or in addition to traditional criminal punishment, such as incarceration or probation.

For a period lasting a minimum of one year, offenders receive treatment and help readjusting to life outside of prison and without drug use. Participants are randomly drug tested and regularly appear before a judge to review their progress. They can be sanctioned or rewarded based on such behavioral criteria as attending meetings, staying drug free and working.

A number of states spend as much or more money on their corrections as they do on higher education.

Drug courts are a relatively recent phenomenon. The number of drug courts has increased from zero in 1988 to more than 2,000 in 2008. The federal government is a major funder of the courts, spending $40 million on them in fiscal year 2009. Many say that drug courts save taxpayers money and are more effective than prison alone. But is that true?

The High Cost of Imprisonment

After almost three decades of growth, the U.S. prison population reached 2.3 million in 2007. This large prison population comes with a hefty price tag. In 2007, the United States spent $44 billion on the prison system—four times (or $33 billion) more than in 1987. The average annual cost of incarceration is $24,000 per inmate. A number of states spend as much or more money on their corrections system as they do on higher education, including Connecticut, Vermont, Delaware, Oregon and Michigan.

The Rate of Drug Use Among Criminals

More than 60 percent of those arrested test positive for alcohol or some type of drug. Some 80 percent of convicted criminals abuse drugs or alcohol, and more than 50 percent can be defined as clinically addicted. Prison itself does little to curb drug abuse:

- In 2004, about 21 percent of prisoners were in jail for a drug-related offense—this percentage has not changed since 1994.

- More than half of inmates will return to prison within three years of their release.

- Even if they do not return to prison, 95 percent of convicts will return to drug use.

Similarly, probation, which is often considered an alternative to incarceration, is not an effective deterrent to drug use. Between 50 percent and 70 percent of probationers fail to comply with drug testing and treatment requirements, which only subjects them to more jail time at taxpayer expense.

Managing an offender through drug court costs more than probation alone, but much less than jail or prison.

The Effectiveness of Drug Courts

Professors at the University of Pennsylvania found that drug courts had a compliance rate six times higher than any other current method of treating criminals with drug addictions. They also found that drug courts were two to three times more successful than other methods in reducing recidivism, drug use and unemployment.

Studies have also shown that drug users who have children are more likely to complete a drug court program than any other type of treatment. Among families whose children have been taken away because of their parents' drug use, reunification rates are 50 percent higher if a parent completes a drug court program, and those children spend less time, on average, in out-of-home placements.

Drug Courts Save Money

According to the National Association of Drug Court Professionals, cost savings due to drug courts range from $4,000 to more than $12,000 per client. Nationwide, for every dollar invested in drug courts, taxpayers save as much as $3.36 in avoided criminal justice costs alone.

A 30-month U.S. Department of Justice study of Portland, Oregon's Multnomah County Drug Court, the second oldest in the nation, found that it saved almost $5,000 per participant, on average, totaling more than $1.5 million per year. The net savings included the actual cost of judges, courtrooms and drug tests, avoided trials and jail time, and avoided victimization costs, such as lost work days, medical expenses and so forth.

Managing an offender through drug court costs more than probation alone, but much less than jail or prison. According to a statewide evaluation of drug court programs in Kentucky:

- In 2004, it cost an average of $1,256 per year for an offender on traditional probation.

- It cost $3,083 to manage an offender through drug court, including administrative and treatment costs.

- By contrast, the one year cost of maintaining an offender in jail was $9,676 or $17,194 in prison.

The Need for More Drug Courts

The U.S. Department of Justice recently identified 1.2 million people in the criminal justice system who would be eligible for drug court but do not have access due to their location.

According to estimates from the National Association of Drug Court Professionals:

- Drug court programs only serve about half of those who qualify, and less than 10 percent of those arrestees at risk for drug and alcohol abuse who would benefit.

- If the programs treated all currently eligible individuals, it would save $2.14 for every $1 invested, totaling $1.17 billion annually.

- Furthermore, if drug courts were expanded to treat all arrestees at risk for drug or alcohol abuse or dependence, it would save an estimated $3.36 for every $1 invested, totaling an additional $32.3 billion annually.

Given the success of drug courts, and the projected savings if more programs were implemented, the United States should use drug courts to save taxpayers' money and effectively treat criminals with drug problems.

5

Drug Courts Are Not Effective for All Offenders

Justice Policy Institute

The Justice Policy Institute is a national nonprofit organization that aims to advance policies that promote well-being and justice for all people and communities.

While drug courts are often promoted as an effective alternative to prison, many factors are never discussed when considering their effectiveness. Drug courts, for instance, are allowed to choose who will enter a given program. By choosing low-level offenders, drug courts guarantee higher success. This methodology, however, unfairly discards many individuals with low incomes or minorities who might benefit from drug court programs. Furthermore, most people who enter drug court programs never complete them. When this happens, the individual often receives a harsher sentence than he or she would have received initially for the crime committed. Drug courts should be reformed to serve everyone. Furthermore, more money should be invested into community programs that prevent individuals with drug problems from ever entering the criminal justice system.

Drug courts that receive federal discretionary grants are required to focus on people accused of nonviolent offenses and those without a violent record. Yet research shows that drug courts have the greatest benefit for people who have more prior felony convictions and have previously failed other dispositions. The Urban Institute's Justice Policy Center estimated that of the 1.5 million people arrested for a drug offense who are at risk of substance abuse or dependence, just over 109,900—about 7 percent—met current eligibility requirements for drug court, and only about half were enrolled in a drug court program. Note that not everyone arrested for a drug offense uses or abuses drugs, and treatment may not be an appropriate option for everyone arrested for a drug offense.

Drug Courts Are Selective

Since people of color are more likely to have a felony conviction on their record at the time of an arrest related to drug abuse, they are more likely to be excluded from consideration for drug court participation. There is also some evidence that sanctions are higher for people of color who violate the rules of the drug court program, and that African Americans are less likely to graduate from drug court than whites—in some courts African Americans are 30 percent more likely than whites to be dropped from the program.

A driving force behind "cherry picking" is the need to show success. If a program doesn't work, it may be defunded. By picking the easier cases—people without prior or significant criminal records and with lesser addictions—courts are able to ensure more success and continuation of the program. As people with the fewest previous convictions and those with "lesser" addictions are the most likely to succeed, the number of graduates and success rates look better for courts that focus on this population. This leaves the people who may benefit most from drug court without access to treatment to help them live a successful life. If courts accept people with more challenging situations or addictions, they will have to adjust their requirements, treatment options and sanctions to best meet their needs.

Drug Courts Are Not Helpful to the Disadvantaged

A number of studies have examined the social and demographic factors associated with success or failure in drug court. Most studies say that people with more resources are more likely to succeed in drug court and that those who are unemployed or under-educated tend to do worse.

Most of the people who start drug court do not successfully complete it.

Studies also found that age correlates with drug court retention—those who are older do better. A report from the Urban Institute found that the oldest participants have the best outcomes. These findings may have further implications for youth who participate in juvenile drug courts rather than receiving community-based treatment. The same study from the Urban Institute also found that whites have lower rates of recidivism after graduating from a drug court program than people of color, indicating that race may also be a factor in successful completion of drug court, although this may be more related to social factors than race or ethnicity.

One of the reasons why people of color and those from poorer communities may be less likely to be accepted into drug court or successfully complete drug court is their increased likelihood of being arrested, which can lead to program termination. People from poorer communities and communities of color are more likely to be under some sort of police surveillance, whether they are under criminal justice control or not. This increased surveillance can lead to more arrests and dismissal from drug court.

Drug Courts Have High Failure Rates

Despite some notable successes in drug court, the vast majority of drug courts have high failure rates—most of the people who start drug court do not successfully complete it. A study by the Government Accountability Office found that drug court graduation rates generally range from about one in four to about two in three. While graduating from a drug court may result in an expungement—but not overall deletion—of a criminal conviction, failing drug court leads to both a criminal conviction and possibly a harsher sentence—including a possible prison sentence—than a participant would have received had he not attempted and failed drug court.

Collateral consequences of conviction

Having a felony conviction on your record, whether it is for a drug offense or other offense, can be extremely detrimental to a person's future. People with criminal records are frequently discriminated against in the work place, and often face housing discrimination and loss of public benefits. Students who receive a drug conviction can be barred from receiving federal financial aid for their education. People who are kicked out of a post-plea drug court will be convicted on the original offense and face a number of these collateral consequences.

Providing treatment in the community before a person becomes involved in the criminal justice system can be an effective way to defeat a problem before it starts.

Harsher sentences

Research and personal accounts of drug court participants and their lawyers show that many people who fail drug courts receive harsher sentences from judges than they would have originally received if they'd never tried and failed at drug court. Although very few studies compare the outcomes of drug court participants who fail to people traditionally adjudicated, evidence from some drug courts suggests that people who fail drug courts receive longer sentences—in some cases even two to five times longer—than people who never attempted drug court.

Drug Court Recommendations

The research and data show that providing treatment in the community has better outcomes and is more cost-effective than treatment in the criminal justice system for people with addictions. Expanding access to treatment outside the justice system to people who need it can help increase public safety, save money and improve life outcomes for individuals. Policymakers should expand treatment services through the public health system so people can get the help they need without having to be arrested. Changing the way we think about drug use and drug policies that bring so many people into the justice system can have a positive and lasting impact on individuals, families and communities.

Invest in front-end treatment and services. Providing treatment in the community before a person becomes involved in the criminal justice system can be an effective way to defeat a problem before it starts. Community-based treatment is truly an investment in public safety, one that will reduce incarceration and its economic and social costs.

Implement "real" diversion policies and alternatives to incarceration. Largely as a result of increasing prison and jail populations, states and localities across the country created or are in the process of implementing diversion programs that keep people—mostly those convicted of low-level and drug offenses—out of jail and prison.

- *California* has been using these programs for a decade through the Proposition 36 program, which diverts people with first- and second-time drug offenses to treatment rather than prison. Prop. 36 participants have outcomes similar to drug court participants and the program has been shown to save an estimated $2,861 per participant, while having no adverse effects on public safety.

- *South Carolina* passed a bill last year authorizing probation and other alternatives to incarceration for people convicted of a first or second time drug offenses. The package is estimated to save $350 million, the cost of building a new prison which would otherwise be necessary.

- *Hawaii* passed a bill a few years ago that created diversion programs for people convicted of first-time, nonviolent drug offenses, and was also made treatment available for people convicted of first-time, nonviolent property offenses whose offense was considered a result of a drug problem. A person sentenced under this law may petition for expungement of their record after successful completion of treatment and probation.

- *Colorado* passed a bill last year emphasizing diversion to substance abuse and mental health treatment for people charged with low-level drug possession.

- *Texas* has been making a number of reforms in recent years, including a bill in 2003 that required that all people convicted of drug possession with less than a gram of drugs be sentenced to probation instead of incarceration. In 2007, the state's budget allocated $241 million for residential and non-residential treatment-oriented programs for people convicted of nonviolent offenses, along with enhancing in-prison treatment programs.

Collect better data on drug courts. National level data on drug court participation and success is hard to come by, making national evaluations of the effectiveness of drug court difficult to measure. More data can lead to better evaluations and recommendations for best practices in drug court, and provide policymakers with information necessary to choose where to spend scarce funds.

Focus court treatment programs on those who would have gone to prison. If a person would have received a prison sentence, then a drug court program can act as a true diversion, saving the state money and protecting public safety through a more intensive period that includes both treatment and supervision.

Evaluate current drug court policies and practices. Drug court administrators should continuously evaluate policies on participant eligibility that may lead to "cherry picking" and practices that lead to higher failure rates for certain groups, especially those with lower income or people of color. More evaluation will lead to more fair and effective programs.

6

Mental Health Courts Are Effective in Reducing Recidivism

Emma Schwartz

Emma Schwartz served as the legal correspondent for US News and World Report *and also writes for the* Huffington Post.

Mental health courts work much like drug courts: they are specifically designed to serve a population with mental health issues. As with drug courts, mental health courts operate on the state level and choose a number of methods of dealing with convicted individuals with mental health issues. While some programs have been accused of being too lenient, traditional prison sentences often seem counterproductive for many mental health problems. Although critics of the mental health court system insist that reforms are needed, many individuals believe that the current system—even if it is imperfect—has offered them a second chance.

Judge John Zottola's courtroom often feels more like a kindergarten award ceremony than part of the criminal justice system. Every Thursday on the fifth floor of a Romanesque-style courthouse, defendants shuffle to a podium to receive compliments, encouragement, and applause, whether it's for sticking to their treatment, wearing a nice outfit, or staying clean and sober. Even defendants who've slipped up on probation are unlikely to be thrown back in jail. Instead, most face a stern but kind warning, along with orders for more rigorous treatment or reporting schedules. "Don't make me look bad," Zottola tells them.

A soft touch is hardly standard for judges. But this is the Allegheny County Mental Health Court, an alternative to traditional criminal court, and it is precisely that sort of approach that has helped keep more and more mentally ill offenders out of jail. "Some people say, 'Is warm and fuzzy appropriate for the criminal justice system?'" says Zottola, a former county prosecutor. "But it really works."

For years, courts have treated the mentally ill with the same dispassion accorded any other defendant. The results have been devastating. More than twice as many people with mental illness live in prisons as in state mental hospitals. When they are confined to tiny cells, their conditions often worsen, increasing their propensity to act out. As a result, the mentally ill face disproportionately harsher discipline than do other inmates behind bars. A 2003 Human Rights Watch report said there were "deep-rooted patterns of neglect, mistreatment and even cavalier disregard for the well-being" of mentally ill inmates.

A New Kind of Court

That attitude is slowly starting to change. Spurred by growing prison populations and high levels of recidivism, mental health courts now number about 175 nationwide. The premise is simple: Instead of being sentenced to jail or standard probation, defendants in mental health court are diverted to treatment programs and remain under regular supervision for a fixed length of time. After going through the Pittsburgh court, which started in 2001, only 10 percent of 223 graduates were rearrested, far below the 68 percent national average for all defendants.

"There are people who are mentally ill who do dangerous and violent things who should not be getting a pass because they are mentally ill," says Douglas Brawley, chief assistant for the mental health court in Broward County, Fla. "But many of the crimes, when you look at them, are manifestations of their mental illness."

Participation in the Pittsburgh program is voluntary. Only a handful of eligible defendants turn it down each year, usually because of the possibility of longer periods of court supervision or long waits for a bed in a treatment facility. While the program accepts those facing misdemeanor and felony charges, it bars sex offenders and most violent criminals. In exchange for their guilty pleas, defendants are put on probation and given a treatment plan. They also receive two months' rent and $200 for new clothing.

Some judges see jail time as fair punishment for breaking treatment; others say jail is counterproductive.

When she first appeared in Zottola's court, Tina Haddix was, to say the least, troubled. Now 35, Haddix had begun drinking at age 12 and was addicted to crack cocaine by her early 20s. Combined with untreated bipolar disorder and depression, her addiction only worsened. Haddix began stealing to feed her habit and soon found herself in jail. In 2005, Haddix was caught forging the checks of her parents and other elderly people. Facing more serious charges, she pleaded guilty to misdemeanor theft and signed up for mental health court.

After a few months in residential treatment, Haddix moved to a halfway house for a year, then signed a lease for her own apartment. During her two years on probation, Haddix never slipped up. By the time she graduated from the court last fall, she had gotten financial aid to take classes to become a drug and alcohol counselor. She says she is certain about where she would be without the mental health court: "Dead or out on the street."

Mental Health Court Success Rates

Not all mental health courts have been as successful as the court in Pittsburgh or the courts in San Francisco and Broward County, where studies have also pointed to lower recidivism rates. Different courts use different treatment facilities. They also apply different sanctions. Some judges see jail time as fair punishment for breaking treatment; others say jail is counterproductive. A number of courts will take felony cases, while others restrict participation to those accused or misdemeanors. "What's unclear is for whom and under what circumstances mental health courts work," says Henry Steadman, the director of Policy Research Associates, who is running the first national study of mental health courts. (Even in Pittsburgh, of the 481 people who have enrolled in the court, 47 have been thrown out or left.)

The courts have sparked criticism by some mental health experts. First, they worry that the courts criminalize the mentally ill because most force defendants to plead guilty in order to receive treatment. (A few will erase charges altogether if treatment is successful.) Second, critics are concerned that the courts divert limited treatment resources from the general community to those with criminal records. "Nobody talks about the trade-offs," says Joseph De Raismes, vice president for public policy for Mental Health America, an advocacy group. "Nobody talks about whether three or four needy people didn't get into treatment."

Mental Health and Drug Addiction

The choices inside court aren't always easy either. During a recent session, Zottola heard the difficult case of Jeffrey Woods, who at age 48 had spent more of his life inside the criminal justice system than outside it. He was raised by a single mother as one of 13 children. Arrested at 17 for stealing from a jewelry store, Woods says he fell into drug dealing for most of his 20s and soon became his own best client. The addiction was heightened by his untreated mental illness: schizoaffective disorder, which had led to a number of suicide attempts. In 1992, he was sent to prison for a decade.

Released in 2003, Woods tried to turn his life around. He fell in love and began to reacquaint himself with his teenage son. But soon, he says, "my urge and needs came back." In 2004 he was arrested again for stealing, but this time, he was offered a way to avoid jail: the mental health court.

Since joining the program, Woods has been charged with four new offenses, including felony theft charges. After his arrest last fall for stealing a $400 watch, he stopped checking in with his probation officer and his therapist. Prosecutor Heather Kelly wanted him thrown out of the program.

Woods, aware that he was on thin ice, had made a preemptive strike by sending the judge a Christmas card. He had also begun showing up for therapy and arrived at court early, clean, and sober. It wasn't perfect, but it was progress. Zottola warned Woods that he was getting close to jail time again. "You have to try to straighten some of this stuff out," the judge said. "I'm ready," Woods assured him, announcing his efforts to enroll in culinary school.

The judge ordered Woods to report for weekly drug tests and to check in regularly with his probation officers. "I have a lot of faith in you," he told the defendant, while reminding him that jail still loomed.

After the hearing, Woods said he feared returning to jail largely because it would cost him his fiancée. But he believes the mental health court has made a difference. "It helps me realize you do have choices in life," he says. Yet he says he's never quite sure what the next moment will hold. When he's off medication, he says, trouble lurks. Last winter he walked out of mental health court, only to be arrested hours later for shoplifting a pair of gloves.

Still, Woods counts himself lucky. He's nearly 50—an age, he says, that his father never reached.

7

Boot Camps Can Be an Effective Alternative to Prison for Adults

Andy Hoag

Andy Hoag is a writer for the Saginaw (MI) News.

One alternative to prison that is used less frequently today is boot camp. Boot camps offer programs in an isolated setting that require discipline, physical conditioning, and classes. While boot camps are less popular now, a number of officials continue to believe that these programs provide a good alternative for certain individuals. The boot camp in Chelsea, Michigan, for instance, serves 1,200–1,400 hundred people a year, and offers classes in drug addiction, decision making, and journaling. While the program is not right for everyone, a number of graduates have attested that boot camp proved successful when other programs had failed. Unfortunately, the program in Chelsea, like many state programs, has been threatened by state budget cuts. Without the program, however, the state would be forced to build expensive prisons to take the place of the boot camp.

Shelly L. Garno was 25 last summer when she gave birth to her son in prison.

The then-St. Charles resident was about seven months pregnant last May when Saginaw County Circuit Judge Fred L. Borchard sentenced her to prison for twice violating the probation she was on for a May 2007 cocaine possession conviction.

Last month, Garno told a group that included Borchard and fellow Circuit Judge Darnell Jackson and state Department of Corrections officials that she was "resentful" when Borchard sentenced her to two to four years. But instead of sending her to traditional prison, Borchard placed Garno in the corrections department's Special Alternative Incarceration [SAI] facility in Chelsea, 20 miles west of Ann Arbor.

"I was mad at Judge Borchard because I thought it was his fault, but it wasn't," she told the group. "I'm a different person now."

The rehabilitation program—singular in the state—that helped Garno faces the possibility of closure because of state budget woes. The program's supporters say it saves money compared to traditional incarceration and reduces recidivism.

Borchard said he'd like to continue to send prisoners there.

"If they don't keep it, it's not going to be beneficial," Borchard said. "We'd be losing the opportunity to turn some of these people around."

A Second 'Chance' for Rehabilitation

Garno named her son Chance because, she said, "I feel like everybody deserves a second chance."

The state's lone remaining adult boot camp, where Garno shared her story, has transformed into a "therapeutic community" with a 90-day program focused on changing negative behavior into socially acceptable behavior, said Deputy Warden Frederic J. Goff.

Two things contributed to Garno's about-face, she told the judges. The first: She spent just three days with her son after she gave birth to him before handing the baby over to his father so she could continue her sentence. Second, Special Alternative Incarceration's emphasis on behavior instead of an in-your-face boot camp philosophy worked for her.

"I didn't see the point in goals, because I knew I wasn't going to accomplish them anyway," she said. "I was going down a dead-end road, constantly messing up."

"You never like locking people up, but she reached the point where you have to protect society and get her attention," said Borchard, who talked privately with Garno after she addressed the group. "I had concerns about her child, and this seemed to be the best answer for her."

No 'Summer Camp'

Garno entered Special Alternative Incarceration on Dec. 30, made it through the 90 days without "messing up" her last chance, and graduated from the facility March 30. With her graduation, Garno is now on parole, just as if she had already served the minimum term of her sentence and earned her parole.

Make no mistake, though: Just because Garno wasn't constantly participating in physical training doesn't mean the program is a cake walk now. . . .

The state created the program in 1988 as one of about a handful of boot camps in the state. First for male probationers only, it expanded to include female prisoners and probationers in 1992. To be eligible, prisoners must be serving their first prison term with a minimum length of no longer than three years. There also is a list of certain crimes the trainees must not have committed, including sexual assault offenses and specific types of assault.

Several of the boot camps were in northern Michigan, but state officials felt that while "utilizing a boot camp concept continued to be good idea, having multiple boot camps or boot camps that were geographically segregated from the majority of the population or judges that would utilize them was counterproductive," said corrections department spokesman John Cordell.

State officials consolidated the camps and maintained the Chelsea facility, which had about 320 trainees enrolled last month and serves 1,200 to 1,400 per year. The facility continued to function as a boot camp until state officials started the Michigan Prisoner ReEntry Initiative, aimed at not only helping prisoners avoid prison but making sure that when they re-entered their communities they wouldn't commit crimes that send them back there.

Any reservations that I had that it [boot camp] would be like summer camp, it wasn't.

"As we continued rolling out different aspects of prisoner re-entry programs, we realized that utilizing the boot camp philosophy wasn't working," Cordell said. "Those offenders weren't significantly more successful than someone who did go to prison."

When Borchard was appointed probate judge in 1998, he visited the boot camp to better understand the system.

"There was a lot more physical punishment in the past, but I don't know if that's going to change anybody, except make them stronger," he said.

With the emphasis on rehabilitation, the rumor among criminal justice workers was that Special Alternative Incarceration had turned into a summer camp where the trainees sat side by side and sang "Kumbaya."

Boot Camp Structure

But boot camp structure and discipline remains. Each instructor goes by "corporal," and almost every statement to the trainees in class, at lunch, or during their duties is followed by a "Yes sir!" or "Yes ma'am!" Trainees must walk as close as they can along the walls, walk in straight, single-file lines, and run when told to run. They're up by 6 a.m. and in bed by 10 p.m., where they share a bunk bed with a roommate and are required to keep their room spotless and their foot lockers uniform and organized.

The officials also have established a detailed disciplinary structure. A demerit results in extra duties, such as cleaning; multiple demerits result in "case notes"; and multiple case notes result in a trip to the Special Alternative Incarceration Review Board. In the midst of the demerit and case note process is what the deputy warden calls motivational detail, which includes more running, work and chopping wood, all while fitting in classes they're still required to attend.

If the motivational detail is unsuccessful, probationers go back for a probation violation hearing before the judge who sent them there, and prisoners are placed back in prison on their original sentence.

"Any reservations that I had that it would be like summer camp, it wasn't," Borchard said. "I was impressed by the programs to help these young men and women."

Jackson also had his doubts about the philosophy but left impressed.

"They take a holistic approach, which I like to see," he said. "I don't want to coddle the prisoners, but we do need to rehabilitate them."

Touring the facility and sitting in on classes showed Jackson that the prisoners were motivated, he said.

"What that (motivation) was was hard to discern, but they're motivated to be there," he said.

Back to School

Still, not everybody makes it through, Goff said.

"A lot of them are tired of being failures but don't know how to be a success," the deputy warden told the touring group.

To make rehabilitation successful, Goff said, the state needed to ensure the communities had a stake in the process.

By providing money and grants to community-based pro-grams such as the Salvation Army and others, the state gave the prisoners an avenue to aid their re-entry process and gave those organizations and communities an incentive to help them.

With the old system, Goff told the group, trainees were not classified by offense or what type of special programming they might require.

"Regardless of whether they had a substance abuse prob-lem, the trainees would go into eight weeks of substance abuse education," Goff said. "The evidence shows that they'll come out (of the camp) with more knowledge about controlled substances. The same goes for anger management."

The trainees are required to keep a journal for their 90-day stay, keeping a log of some of the decisions they make every day.

Today, trainees are classified at the Egeler Reception and Guidance Center in Jackson. After three weeks of training—including learning the seven basic rules, such as when to talk and how—they are placed in the classes that address their specific issues.

Those classes include "Pick A Partner," where Cpl. Terry Bridges teaches trainees how to build a solid relationship with a significant other, and "Thinking Matters," where Cpl. Chris Bouldrey shows the trainees how to understand their decision-making and learn from it. The trainees are required to keep a journal for their 90-day stay, keeping a log of some of the de-cisions they make every day and showing how they can apply that to their lives.

Goff said a majority of the 120 staff members are trained in journaling, giving Special Alternative Incarceration a "cul-ture of staff that knows what we're doing" and trying to ac-complish with the journal concept.

Bouldrey's decision-making class was the judges' favorite.

"At some point, nobody decides to become a victim, but someone does decide to break the law," Jackson said.

Understanding those decisions is "real important" for the trainees, Jackson said.

"You really hope that with the two-minute talk you give them (in court), they'll make the right choices," Borchard said. "But with this class, I hope they're making the right choice because they want to."

A Much-Needed Alternative

Borchard and Jackson made the 220-mile round-trip visit because they wanted to witness the new philosophy themselves. Program officials hope the judges also encourage legislators to continue to fund the initiative.

The state Senate's budget recommendation does not have funding for the Chelsea facility, Cordell said.

"Without a 2010–2011 budget that funds SAI, it's wholly and completely possible that it could close," he said. "And that's a difficult situation."

The ability to divert prisoners back into the community with the support of judges really allows us to help control the prison population.

Cordell said the state spends about $11 million a year to run Special Alternative Incarceration.

"But you can't cut out $11 million out of the budget thinking you're going to create $11 million in savings," he said.

Doing so "ultimately will increase the prisoner population by almost 2,000 in the first year and a half. You will have to create bed space for those 2,000 prisoners."

That's the equivalent of about two extra prisons, Cordell said, which would cost $25 million to $30 million apiece annually to run.

"The ability to divert prisoners from that intermediate sort of sentence back into the community with the support of judges really allows us to help control the prison population," Cordell said. "If we take that tool away, we're going to see a prison expansion."

The state's prison population has decreased to about 45,000 since March 2007, when it reached a record high of 51,544.

"And not only would they come to prison, they're coming for a significantly longer time than the 90-day SAI program," Cordell said.

Maintaining funding is what Borchard and Jackson want to see, they said.

"I like the program; I think it's viable," Jackson said. "I'll be more likely to send someone there. If you don't want to overload the prisons, this fits the bill."

8

Shame Punishment Is an Effective Alternative to Incarceration

Albert B. Southwick

Albert B. Southwick writes a column for the Worcester (MA) Telegram and Gazette.

In early American history, shame was often used to deter crime. In a manner similar to the one depicted in Nathaniel Hawthorne's novel The Scarlet Letter, *individuals were publicly humiliated. A pillory, for instance, was sometimes used in the public square, holding the criminal immobile as others passed by and commented. While many of the punishments relied on in the past would be considered too harsh today, reviving public shaming could offer an effective way to deter drunk drivers and other offenders.*

I got to thinking the other day about the people who strain our police departments and clog our courts with their petty and not so petty offenses.

You read about them every day in newspaper coverage of the police and the courts. Repeat offenders are prominent. Whether shoplifting, committing burglaries, getting into fights, dealing drugs or whatnot, they seem to have no moral guidelines in their lives. They are punished in various ways, ranging from prison sentences to probation, from stints of community service to wearing electronic bracelets. Such measures are not 100 percent effective.

I began to wonder whether modern society could make more use of an ancient weapon—shame. For example, what if people convicted of driving drunk more than three times were required to display a prominent "DUI" [Driving Under the Influence] sign on their vehicles. That might get their attention more effectively than a $100 fine, and it would also alert other drivers to take care when around them.

Using Shame to Deter Crime

Shame was a big item in Colonial America and for years after. In Nathaniel Hawthorne's novel *The Scarlet Letter*, Hester Prynne was required to wear a big red letter "A" to denote the fact that she had had a fling with the minister Arthur Dimmesdale. It stood for "adultery," a serious business in those days.

Shame was not the only weapon in the law then. Physical punishment was also on the agenda. According to Herbert M. Sawyer's history of the Worcester [Massachusetts] Police Department, "In the early history of Worcester, crime was frequent and punishment severe . . . The gallows was erected for burglars and murderers alike . . . Offenses which in these times (1900) would furnish no public interest were disposed of with a light fine or a short term of imprisonment in the pillory or at the whipping post."

The pillory was a device with holes for the head and two arms. When it was clamped shut, the malefactor had to stand for an hour or so with his imprisoned head and arms protruding, listening to derisive comments from passers-by.

Mr. Sawyer notes, "It was also a favorite sentence of the court to condemn a prisoner to the gallows for an hour, to sit with a rope around his neck, to give him the opportunity to think about death and his God."

Is it somewhat unsettling to think of that kind of raw, brutal punishment being meted out here in Worcester, the Heart of the Commonwealth. Whipping posts! On Court Hill? Hard to believe.

Tough on Crime

But not only whipping posts. Also branding and mutilation.

"Branding a prisoner on the forehead," noted Mr. Sawyer, "or cropping one of the ears was occasionally included in judicial sentences in cases of burglary."

Burglary in those days was sometimes punished by hanging, although never in Worcester as far as I can find. I don't know if anyone in Worcester was ever branded or had his ears cropped.

OK, so maybe branding and ear cropping are beyond the pale.

There were plenty of misdemeanors to run afoul of. The last bylaws adopted by the town of Worcester in 1838 prohibited ball playing in the public streets, throwing stones in the streets, smoking a cigar or pipe in any of the streets within the school district, swimming in the daytime in the Blackstone Canal "in view of a dwelling house, street or highway," driving faster than 8 miles an hour, and carrying a naked scythe between sunset and sunrise.

Fines for such activities ranged from one to 10 dollars.

I guess I've made my point. Those early Worcesterites had a clear idea of what was right and wrong. No excuses based on one's dismal upbringing or brutal parents.

OK, so maybe branding and ear cropping are beyond the pale. But what about my suggestion that chronic drunks with three DUI convictions be required to have a big DUI sign on their cars?

They, no doubt, would think such a requirement shameful.

But that's the point.

9

Shame Punishment Has Limits as Criminal Justice

Greg Beato

Greg Beato is a San Francisco-based writer.

When mug shots were first used in the late 1800s, they served one purpose: to help law enforcement identify individuals in an age without finger prints or other forms of identification. Today, however, mug shots commonly appear on the Internet and within the pages of cheap magazines, and are available to everyone. The problem is, most mug shots are taken before an individual is tried in the court of law. In essence, making a mug shot public is equal to publicly shaming a person before he or she has been convicted in court. In this fashion, published mug shots of people who have not been convicted of any crime serve as little more than public entertainment at the expense of due process.

Murder rates have dropped during the last decade. Same with rape, robbery, assault, burglary, and theft. Yet somehow we're in the midst of the greatest mug shot epidemic the world has ever known.

Every year, more than 14 million people are arrested in the U.S.—and you've probably seen half of them. On the Web, in newspapers, and over the airwaves, the mug shot is king, the signature form of narrative in the Twitter Age. What else communicates so much specificity and mystery so concisely? What else packs so much into a single image: humor, tragedy, unparalleled guidance on which neck tattoos to avoid? It doesn't hurt that mug shots can still deliver the illicit charge that comes with nonconsensual disclosure. Sure, there are a few beaming boozeheads and upbeat probation violators who spoil the mood by, well, mugging for the cameras. But most mug shot subjects look profoundly unexcited to be starring in their very own episode of *Punk'd: Law Enforcement Edition*. Amid our current plague of recidivist exhibitionists, such reticence is a rare commodity. Who isn't going to look?

Today mug shots are still used to identify, but we also want them to punish, deter, and entertain.

Public Shaming

An ever-growing number of law enforcement agencies and media outlets are happy to capitalize on our voyeuristic interest. If you want to know which city has cuter hookers, St. Paul or Peoria, their official city websites regularly publish mug shots of recently arrested prostitutes and Johns. (St. Paul wins by a nose.) If you'd like to see who's doing most of the drunk driving or shoplifting on Long Island, *Newsday.com* now maintains an extensive gallery of local arrestees. (Websites for other newspapers, such as the *Chicago Tribune* and the *Los Angeles Times*, have featured *Newsday's* mug shots too, presumably so readers in every part of the country can know whom to avoid if they ever find themselves in Sag Harbor.) Specialized sites such as Mugshots.com and TheSmokingGun.com curate their collections with a more discerning eye, featuring only the famous, or those with defiantly unrepentant hair, or those who, in addition to all the usual traumas and humiliations that come with arrest, have the misfortune of being heckled by their own clothing during their mug shot sessions. Smile, grim-looking sexual predator in the World's Greatest Dad T-shirt: You're about to become famous!

In the 1880s, when a French crime fighter named Alphonse Bertillon pioneered the mug shot as a unique form of portraiture, the photographs he took were expected to do one thing: Help establish an individual's identity at a time when driver's licenses, fingerprint files, and Facebook pages didn't exist. Today mug shots are still used to identify, but we also want them to punish, deter, and entertain. Unfortunately, they do such a good job of the latter that we've been indifferent to the ways they short-circuit due process. But while we're gawking at the haunted eyes of a Midwestern meth freak or the haunted hair of Nick Nolte, cops across America are using virtual rogues' galleries to normalize the idea that the government has the right to punish you without bothering to convict you of a crime.

Perhaps because mug shots don't need much value adding from would-be Pulitzer winners to capture a reader's attention, publishing them is not the shortest path to praise from journalistic elites. Yet what informed citizen isn't interested in knowing exactly who's getting arrested in his neighborhood, and for what? In the crowning example of mug shot proliferation, the last decade has seen the creation of numerous ink-on-wood-pulp newspapers devoted exclusively to the form, with names like *Gotch-ya!*, *Busted*, *Cellmates*, and *The Slammer*. They're typically founded by undercapitalized entrepreneurs with little or no prior experience in the newspaper business. They're most often distributed at gas stations, liquor stores, and corner markets in the sort of neighborhoods more likely to be featured on *Cops* than HGTV. They go for $1 apiece, and at a time when traditional newspapers can barely give their products away, they're selling like hotcakes.

Short-Changing the Legal Process

Local MugSHOTS is the Gannett Group of the genre. Introduced in 2000, the 12-page tabloid features 250 to 300 mug shots per issue. Dozens of county-specific versions appear in

10 states now. Its publisher, who goes by the name Max Cannon, says approximately 250,000 copies in all are printed for the various biweekly editions, and that some counties have print runs of as high as 20,000.

Thanks to those 14 million annual arrestees, there is plenty of room for growth. But are all mug shots fit to print? Public shaming may represent a cost-effective alternative to traditional forms of sentencing, and as public shaming goes, having your mug shot appear on a police department website actually sounds a lot more agreeable than, say, standing outside a Walgreen's with a sign identifying you as a shoplifter.

Mug shots have always carried the heavy suggestion of guilt.

If you do end up in front of that Walgreen's, however, you've also spent some time in front of a judge or jury, who ultimately found you guilty. With mug shots, that's not necessarily the case. The city of St. Paul, Minnesota, which started publishing photographs of prostitution arrestees in print in the 1980s and brought its operation to the Web in 1997, is regarded as the pioneer of online public humiliation. Following the city's lead, an ever-expanding list of law enforcement agencies now post mug shots of the people they arrest—but don't necessarily convict—in an explicit effort to deter crime.

In general, mug shots have always carried the heavy suggestion of guilt, as if getting caught in the act of being arrested is tantamount to getting caught in the act of committing a crime. It isn't, though, and that's one reason why until relatively recently, many law enforcement agencies, including those operated by the federal government, were reluctant to release mug shots to the press or the public. Indeed, in 1905 a New York City magistrate named Alfred E. Ommen was so concerned about exposing the head shots of possibly innocent citizens to the "public gaze" that he argued, in the pages of the

Journal of Social Science, that "it ought to be a misdemeanor for the Police Department to photograph or measure a man merely charged with a crime."

If there's a chance that the people on display haven't committed a crime, why are they being punished?

Public Voyeurism

While few of Ommen's colleagues in the law enforcement world seemed to share his opinion, until 10 years ago or so it typically took a Freedom of Information Act request, or in extreme cases a lawsuit, to expose a mug shot to the public gaze. In the Internet era, that has changed radically. In 1996 Peoria police refused to grant access to its mug shots until it was sued by a local attorney who wanted to publish photos of people who'd been arrested for soliciting prostitutes. By 2005 the Peoria Police Department had started publishing photos of arrested Johns and prostitutes itself, on the city's official website.

Like most of these sites, Peoria's is careful to include a disclaimer that the individuals depicted on it are "presumed innocent until proven guilty in a court of law." But if there's a chance that the people on display there haven't committed a crime, why are they being punished? As soon as a law enforcement agency presents its online rogues' gallery as a form of deterrence, it transforms the pictures into a form of punishment as well. If appearing in this context is a fate so unpleasant that it can persuade other people to avoid engaging in illicit behavior, then surely it constitutes a penalty. And it's a penalty that's being applied without the hassle of due process.

We tend to overlook this fact because, frankly, it spoils the mood. The presumption of guilt makes it easier to justify laughing at 23-going-on-zombie crack whores and bugeyed misfits sporting felony-caliber mullets. They deserve the derision they get—they're criminals! But the joke is really on us. As law enforcement agencies expand their powers of surveillance, as they encourage us to think of punishment without due process as standard operating procedure, we not only tolerate it, we click and click and ask for more. If America's citizenry were more uniformly presentable, and its mug shots correspondingly less entertaining, we might protest these developments more strongly. Instead, we simply laugh at the latest person guilty of wearing a cow costume while being arrested, then pass along the link to our friends.

10

Electronic Monitoring and Intensive Probation Reduce Recidivism

Graeme Wood

Graeme Wood has been writing for the Atlantic *since 2006.*

Recently, electronic devices with GPS (global positioning system) capacity have been used to track criminals outside of prison. These systems, along with "swift and certain" parole programs, offer the possibility of "prisons without walls." The United States currently has over two million criminals in jail, even though half of these are nonviolent offenders. Unfortunately, prison frequently seems to be a training ground for repeat offenders: the harsh life within prison does little to alter problems with impulse control. With GPS tracking systems attached to individuals and parole programs with strict oversight, nonviolent criminals can continue to live a mostly normal life that allows them to contribute to society. Furthermore, this approach costs much less than traditional imprisonment. While critics worry that some criminals will simply remove ankle bracelets and continue to commit crimes, the worry seems overstated. These new alternatives to prison may not solve every problem in the criminal justice system, but they do offer the chance to reform many criminals, something the current system seems incapable of.

One snowy night last winter, I walked into a pizzeria in Morrisville, Pennsylvania, with my right pant leg hiked up my shin. A pager-size black box was strapped to my sockless ankle, and another, somewhat larger unit dangled in a holster on my belt. Together, the two items make up a tracking device called the BI ExacuTrack AT: the former is designed to be tamper-resistant, and the latter broadcasts the wearer's location to a monitoring company via GPS [global positioning system]. The device is commonly associated with paroled sex offenders, who wear it so authorities can keep an eye on their movements. Thus my experiment: an online guide had specified that the restaurant I was visiting was a "family" joint. Would the moms and dads, confronted with my anklet, identify me as a possible predator and hustle their kids back out into the cold?

Increasingly, GPS devices are looking like an appealing alternative to conventional incarceration.

Well, no, not in this case. Not a soul took any notice of the gizmos I wore. The whole rig is surprisingly small and unobtrusive, and it allowed me to eat my slice in peace. Indeed, over the few days that I posed as a monitored man, the closest I came to feeling a real stigma was an encounter I had at a Holiday Inn ice machine, where a bearded trucker type gave me a wider berth than I might otherwise have expected. All in all, it didn't seem like such a terrible fate.

Unlike most of ExacuTrack's clientele, of course, I wore my device by choice and only briefly, to find out how it felt and how people reacted to it. By contrast, a real sex offender—or any of a variety of other lawbreakers, including killers, check bouncers, thieves, and drug users—might wear the unit or one like it for years, or even decades. He (and the offender is generally a "he") would wear it all day and all night, into the shower and under the sheets—perhaps with an

AC adapter cord snaking out into a wall socket for charging. The device would enable the monitoring company to follow his every move, from home to work to the store, and, in consultation with a parole or probation officer, to keep him away from kindergartens, playgrounds, Jonas Brothers concerts, and other places where kids congregate. Should he decide to snip off the anklet (the band is rubber, and would succumb easily to pruning shears), a severed cable would alert the company that he had tampered with the unit, and absent a very good excuse he would likely be sent back to prison. Little wonder that the law-enforcement officer who installed my ExacuTrack noted that he was doing me a favor by unboxing a fresh unit: over their lifetimes, many of the trackers become encrusted with the filth and dead skin of previous bearers, some of whom are infected with prison plagues such as herpes or hepatitis. Officers clean the units and replace the straps between users, but I strongly preferred not to have anything rubbing against my ankle that had spent years rubbing against someone else's.

GPS Devices As Prison Alternatives

Increasingly, GPS devices such as the one I wore are looking like an appealing alternative to conventional incarceration, as it becomes ever clearer that, in the United States at least, *traditional prison* has become more or less synonymous with *failed prison*. By almost any metric, our practice of locking large numbers of people behind bars has proved at best ineffective and at worst a national disgrace. According to a recent Pew report, 2.3 million Americans are currently incarcerated—enough people to fill the city of Houston. Since 1983, the number of inmates has more than tripled and the total cost of corrections has jumped sixfold, from $10.4 billion to $68.7 billion. In California, the cost per inmate has kept pace with the cost of an Ivy League education, at just shy of $50,000 a year.

This might make some sense if crime rates had also tripled. But they haven't: rather, even as crime has fallen, the sentences served by criminals have grown, thanks in large part to mandatory minimums and draconian three-strikes rules—politically popular measures that have shown little deterrent effect but have left the prison system overflowing with inmates. The vogue for incarceration might also make sense if the prisons repaid society's investment by releasing reformed inmates who behaved better than before they were locked up. But that isn't the case either: half of those released are back in prison within three years. Indeed, research by the economists Jesse Shapiro of the University of Chicago and M. Keith Chen of Yale indicates that the stated purpose of incarceration, which is to place prisoners under harsh conditions on the assumption that they will be "scared straight," is actively counterproductive. Such conditions—and U.S. prisons are astonishingly harsh, with as many as 20 percent of male inmates facing sexual assault—typically harden criminals, making them *more* violent and predatory. Essentially, when we lock someone up today, we are agreeing to pay a large (and growing) sum of money merely to put off dealing with him until he is released in a few years, often as a greater menace to society than when he went in.

Changing Conventional Prison

Devices such as the ExacuTrack, along with other advances in both the ways we monitor criminals and the ways we punish them for their transgressions, suggest a revolutionary possibility: that we might turn the conventional prison system inside out for a substantial number of inmates, doing away with the current, expensive array of guards and cells and fences, in favor of a regimen of close, constant surveillance on the outside and swift, certain punishment for any deviations from an established, legally unobjectionable routine. The potential upside is enormous. Not only might such a system save billions of dollars annually, it could theoretically produce far better outcomes, training convicts to become law-abiders rather than more-ruthless lawbreakers. The ultimate result could be lower crime rates, at a reduced cost, and with considerably less inhumanity in the bargain.

Compared with incarceration, the cost of surveillance is miniscule.

Moreover, such a change would in fact be less radical than it might at first appear. An underappreciated fact of our penitentiary system is that of all Americans "serving time" at any given moment, only a third are actually behind bars. The rest—some 5 million of them—are circulating among the free on conditional supervised release either as parolees, who are freed from prison before their sentences conclude, or as probationers, who walk free in lieu of jail time. These prisoners-on-the-outside have in fact outnumbered the incarcerated for decades. And recent innovations, both technological and procedural, could enable such programs to advance to a stage where they put the traditional model of incarceration to shame.

In a number of experimental cases, they already have. Devices such as the one I wore on my leg already allow tens of thousands of convicts to walk the streets relatively freely, impeded only by the knowledge that if they loiter by a schoolyard, say, or near the house of the ex-girlfriend they threatened, or on a street corner known for its crack trade, the law will come to find them. Compared with incarceration, the cost of such surveillance is minuscule—mere dollars per day—and monitoring has few of the hardening effects of time behind bars. Nor do all the innovations being developed depend on technology. Similar efforts to control criminals in the wild are under way in pilot programs that demand adherence to onerous parole guidelines, such as frequent, random drug testing, and that provide for immediate punishment if the parolees fail. The result is the same: convicts who might once have been in prison now walk among us unrecognized—like pod people, or Canadians.

More than a fifth of all incarcerated criminals are in for drug offenses.

There are, of course, many thousands of dangerous felons who can't be trusted on the loose. But if we extended this form of enhanced, supervised release even to just the nonviolent offenders currently behind bars, we would empty half our prison beds in one swoop. Inevitably, some of those released would take the pruning-shears route. And some would offend again. But then, so too do those convicts released at the end of their brutal, hardening sentences under our current system. And even accepting a certain failure rate, by nearly any measure such "prisons without bars" would represent a giant step forward for justice, criminal rehabilitation, and society. . . .

"Swift and Certain" Judgement

Criminals typically differ from the broader population in a number of ways, including poor impulse control, addictive personality, and orientation toward short-term gratification rather than long-run consequences. More than a fifth of all incarcerated criminals are in for drug offenses, and a large portion of the others abuse legal and illegal substances. If one were to design a criminal-justice system from scratch with these characteristics in mind, it would be difficult to come up with something less effective than what we have today.

Take the world of supervised release, for example. With some exceptions . . . , parolees and probationers know that if they violate the terms of their release, they are unlikely to be caught—and even less likely to be punished. So, impulsive as many of them are, they will transgress, perhaps modestly at first, but over time with growing recklessness, until many have resumed the criminal habits—drug use, theft, or worse—that got them arrested in the first place.

This prevailing condition is something Mark A. R. Kleiman, a professor of public policy at the University of California at Los Angeles and a leading advocate of non-prison alternatives, calls "randomized severity": some transgressors will be punished for violations, sometimes quite harshly, but others will not be punished at all, whether because their delinquencies go undetected or because judges, police, and parole officers decline to pursue the severe penalties that could apply. In his 2009 book, *When Brute Force Fails*, Kleiman argues that such capricious enforcement undermines efforts to reduce crime, and moreover that tough penalties—such as the long sentences that have contributed to clogged prisons—don't do much to help, despite their high cost. The alternative, Kleiman suggests, is a paradigm called "swift and certain" justice, first proposed by Cesare Beccaria in the 18th century: immediate, automatic penalties—though not necessarily severe ones—doled out by credible, identifiable figures.

A New Kind of Probation

One way to achieve this result is through monitoring devices. . . . But a pioneering judge in Hawaii has demonstrated that it can also be accomplished without the technological assist. In the early 2000s, Steven Alm, a circuit judge in Honolulu, grew increasingly frustrated with what he viewed as a farcical probation system. The majority of the cases he saw were drug-related offenses, including property crimes such as burglaries and thefts from tourists' rental cars. Many of the defendants in his court received probation, but once they were back on the street, they might as well never have been convicted. Drug tests, for instance, were scheduled a full month in advance, even though the test could detect meth use only within the previous three days. Despite this, probationers still tested positive about half of the time, indicating that they couldn't stay clean for even that short interval.

One reason for the backsliding, presumably, was that violators knew that in practice they had little to fear. Probation officers had limited time and resources, and to ask for a convict's probation to be revoked would require a great deal of work. Moreover, officers weren't always eager to send someone to prison for five years just for getting high. Since the probationers viewed the enforcers of their probation as lenient, overworked, and somewhat unpredictable, they correctly assumed there was a good chance they could get away with toking up at will.

Then, in 2004, Judge Alm decided to test the "swift and certain" paradigm. "It's something we always talk about in the sociology classes," he told me. "It just never happens in the criminal-justice system." Alm, a former U.S. attorney who was born in Hawaii, instituted what academics such as Kleiman describe as one of the most innovative and successful alternatives to incarceration in recent years. The basic tenet will be familiar to anyone who has ever trained a puppy: punishment must be consistent and immediate, in order to maintain a clear linkage between transgression and consequences. Alm began by assembling 34 probationers chosen because their profiles suggested they were especially incorrigible. He told them: "Everybody in this courtroom wants you to succeed on probation. But for you not to be in prison means you are making a deal with me to follow the rules. If you don't want to follow the rules, tell me now, and I will send you to prison."

The rules were simple: each probationer had to call in to the courthouse every weekday to find out whether he was required to come in for an observed urine test. These tests occurred frequently, and if a probationer ever failed a test or failed to report for a test or a meeting with his probation officer, he was locked away for two days and hauled before the judge for immediate continued sentencing. The justice system under Alm was a consistent and unforgiving machine, dispensing instant punishment for every transgression. The effect was to make life on the outside a little more like life on the inside, with strict, regular monitoring of everyone in the system. If you used illegal drugs, you would be caught.

Hawaii's HOPE Program

Alm worked with Kevin Takata, a supervisor in the prosecutor's office, to come up with a form that reduced the paperwork time for demanding a probation modification from hours or days to minutes. And rather than require a complete overhaul of the terms of a violator's probation, the judge simply handed down jail time. In practice, the sentences were not especially long—days or weeks, in most cases—but, as Kleiman argues, it was not the duration of punishment but the certainty that was crucial.

The results of Alm's program, called Hawaii's Opportunity Probation with Enforcement, or HOPE, astonished everyone. The probationers shaped up quickly, and over time they showed remarkably little inclination to go astray. The urine tests came back dirty a tenth as often as before. "We discovered that most of these guys can stop using on their own," Alm explained, given the discipline imposed by HOPE. For most probationers, the strict observation was as good as, or better than, any drug-treatment program. It generally took no more than one stint in jail before an offender realized that the consequences of a relapse were real; second violations were unusual. And according to a study co-authored by Kleiman, recidivism—that is, arrests for the commission of new crimes, rather than just violations of probation—dropped by half.

Alm was inherently skeptical that prison is the appropriate remedy for many types of offenses. "You don't want to send a 20-year-old who's driving a stolen car and has a little dope on him when he's caught to prison," he said. "He's not going to come out better. I belong to the school of judge-thought that says we should be sending to prison the people we are afraid of, or who won't stop stealing."

Probation officers started volunteering their problem cases to Alm's court, and now all of his cases—more than 1,300—are HOPE probationers. Still more remarkable, the demands of the program—constant testing, appearances before the judge—have not overwhelmed the court system. Violators come in to see the judge, and attorneys complain about having to show up for hearings over even the smallest violations of probation. But overall, the court's volume of work per offender has declined, as has the cost to the state. "You can get someone out working, versus having the state lock them up at a cost of $35,000 per year," explained Myles Breiner, the president of Hawaii's association of criminal defense lawyers. "Who wants to spend more money on the Corrections Corporation of America?" . . .

There are also, of course, worries about the creeping power of the government, and the routinization of surveillance.

Big Brother Surveillance

There are moves under way to experiment with HOPE-like programs outside Hawaii. In addition to the conversations Alm has held with Attorney General Holder, legislation introduced by Representatives Adam B. Schiff (a California Democrat) and Ted Poe (a Texas Republican) would establish a competitive grant program to provide seed money for HOPE-style probation systems. Small programs are in place in Nevada and Oregon, and Alaska launched its own effort this summer. And the market for monitoring devices seems destined to expand, as the technology involved becomes more widespread and hardware costs continue to fall. Already, I have an application on my iPhone that broadcasts my exact location to selected friends at all times. If I were ever convicted of a crime and forced to submit to GPS tracking, I would, in theory, need only to add my probation officer to my Google Friends list and keep my phone handy. . . . And with prison costs rising, and the pernicious effects of incarceration becoming clearer all the time, the problem of selling prisons without walls will presumably grow easier over time.

There are also, of course, worries about the creeping power of government, and the routinization of surveillance. . . . There is no reason, as the technology gets cheaper and the monitoring ever more fine-grained, why electronic monitoring could not be used to impose an ever wider range of requirements on an ever wider range of "criminals." A serious felon might have every second of his day tracked, whereas a lighter offender like myself—recently caught lead-footed by a traffic camera—might be required to carry a tracker that issues an alert any time I move faster than 65 miles per hour. (If such an intervention sounds far-fetched, recall that many jurisdictions in the United States already require convicted drunk drivers to pass an ignition-mounted Breathalyzer test before they can start their cars.) . . .

Balancing Personal Rights and Surveillance

And what of our rights, those of us outside the realm of the criminal-justice system? If the past several years in the shadow of a war against terrorism have taught us anything, it is that, once available, surveillance technologies rarely go unused, or un-abused. Could yesterday's warrantless wiretapping become tomorrow's clandestine cell-phone tracking? The technology already exists: even a cell phone that lacks a GPS can be traced to within a few city blocks. Once the legal and technical infrastructures were in place to allow the monitoring of criminals, it would be a relatively simple step to extend that monitoring to any person the government considered, for whatever reason, to be "of interest."

For now, of course, none of these scenarios is close to taking place. Even HOPE, a narrow, low-tech program, is limited to Hawaii, and the number of convicts wearing . . . anklets still make up a tiny fraction of those serving time, even outside prison walls. When close monitoring of probationers and parolees emerges as an ever more obvious alternative to expensive incarcerations, we would be wise to remain vigilant against Orwellian abuses. But potential drawbacks and pitfalls notwithstanding, it seems likely that the invasive surveillance model, combining tracking technology and the Kleiman/Alm paradigm of "swift and certain" justice, could offer an alternative to much of the waste—in human as well as economic terms—of our current, dysfunctional system.

If a device strapped to an ankle can help restore balance, can amplify the voice of conscience relative to the others, is that such a bad thing?

In a way, the goal of Panopticon justice is as old as morality itself. It aims to install a tiny voice in each offender's head, a warning that someone is watching and that wrongdoing will be punished. Most of us call that tiny voice a conscience. But for some that voice is overwhelmed by other, louder voices expressing need or impulse or desire, voices less bound by reason or consequence. If a device strapped to an ankle can help restore the balance, can amplify the voice of conscience relative to the others, is that such a bad thing? For optimists of human nature, it is a melancholy realization that the highest function of humanity can be, to some extent, outsourced to a plastic box. But the American criminal-justice system has become in many ways a graveyard of optimism. And surely it is better to outsource the fragile voice of conscience to a plastic box than to do what our brick-and-bar prisons so often do, which is to extinguish that voice altogether.

11

Electronic Monitoring Does Not Prevent Repeat Crimes

London Evening Standard

The London Evening Standard *is a British newspaper.*

In Britain, a number of prisoners have been released early with the condition that they wear an electronic device that allows their movement to be tracked. Unfortunately, statistics have shown that many prisoners wearing electronic tags have committed new crimes, creating a threat to public safety. These crimes include serious offenses, and were often committed following multiple parole violations that went unpunished. Simply stated, electronic tags do not work.

They have committed some of the most appalling crimes possible—despite being under the apparent supervision of an electronic tag.

The offences carried out by these men range from murder to child rape.

All ten were supposed to be monitored by the tags when they reoffended.

Their crimes make a mockery of a pronouncement by Home Office minister Gerry Sutcliffe yesterday that the majority of the public believes that electronic tagging of offenders is a 'good scheme'.

Mr Sutcliffe made his comments on the day new figures revealed that more than 1,000 violent crimes, including five killings, have been committed by prisoners released early with electronic tags.

He told Radio 4's Today programme that less than four per cent of people offended while wearing tags.

'Most people see it as a [British Broadcasting Company] good scheme to help them back into society,' he told the BBC. There has to be a punishment, as far as the sentence is concerned, but there has to be rehabilitation as well.'

Home Detention and Curfew

Under the Home Detention Curfew, prisoners can be released up to four and a half months early, as long as they wear an electronic tag. Prisoners can also be given a tag in lieu of a custodial term.

But the Tories [political party] said it showed a 'shocking disregard for public safety'. Shadow Home Secretary David Davis said the report raised serious questions about the way tagging was being used.

'With so many serious offences being committed it is clear the government is showing a shocking disregard for public safety,' he said.

Liberal Democrat home affairs spokesman Nick Clegg said flaws in the tagging system could be 'laid squarely at the government's feet for failing to implement the system competently in practice'.

Former senior probation officer David Fraser said the government should abandon tagging altogether.

'Supervising persistent offenders in the community, with or without a tag, is disastrous for the public,' he said.

'The public need to be protected from crime. It is absolutely amazing that [the government] are able, somehow, to ignore this. What must happen? They are sleepwalking into civil unrest, in my view.'

Here the *Mail* details ten of the worst reoffenders who have carried out 'tagging crimes' after being released from jail or excused custody altogether:

Peter Williams, 19, from Nottingham Original crime: Burglary. Sentence: 16 months in prison but released after a year with an electronic tag. Crime while tagged: Involved in the September 2003 killing of shopkeeper Marian Bates. Mrs Bates, 64, was shot dead by Williams' accomplice. Williams tore off the tag, ignored six curfews and missed seven probation appointments before the killing.

Steven Readdy, 20, from Manchester. Original crime: burglary and theft Sentence: 60 hour community punishment and tagged. Crime while tagged: In April 2004—three months after being tagged—he raped a girl of 12.

Robert Clegg, 17, from Rochdale Original crime: Stealing a car and carrying a knife and air rifle. Sentence: Tagged and placed under a 9pm curfew. Crime while tagged: Savagely murdered 60 year-old grandfather Bob Boardman by stabbing him more than 30 times in May 2004. Removed his tag before committing the murder and had previously breached the curfew 13 times, without penalty.

He tore off the tag and raped a 38-year-old woman on a canal barge, where he held her prisoner for seven hours.

Elias Cecchetti, 15, from North London Original crime: Assault. Sentence: One year supervision order. Crime while tagged: Attacked teacher Monica Watts in December 2003 with a six-inch knife as the 39-year-old was jogging. Ceccheti—nicknamed 'Slasher'—was under a curfew and wearing a tag as he awaited trial for robbery.

John Davis, 20, from Slough. Berkshire Original crime: handling stolen goods. Sentence: 18 months. Crime while tagged: Davis was part of a gang which tried to snatch $90 million in gold, diamonds and cash at Heathrow in September last year. He had been released early with a tag.

Andrew Wild, 40, from Bury Original crime: assault. Sentence: five years. Crime while tagged: In April last year he was released on parole with an electronic tag. Two months later he tore off the tag and raped a 38-year-old woman on a canal barge, where he held her prisoner for seven hours.

Callum Evans, 18, from Glasgow Original crime: Assault and robbery. Sentence: Tagged for two months. Crime while tagged: Murdered 23-year-old John Hatfield outside a block of flats in October 2005. Wearing a tag at the time, but the alarm did not sound as he was within the tag's 'detection' range.

William Steward, 27, from London Original crime: driving while banned and dangerous driving. Sentence: 18 weeks. Crime while tagged: Within days of his release in November 2002 he raped a businesswoman in her five-star Brighton hotel room.

David Sudlow, 60, from Warrington Original Crime: Possessing and attempting to supply drugs. Sentence: 12 months. Crime while tagged: He was freed in January 2000 after just four months in prison. A month later he removed his tag and raped a 14-year-old girl after plying her with drugs and alcohol.

Paul May, 32, from Newport, Wales Original Crime: wounding in April 2003. Sentence: 18 months in prison. Crime while tagged: In November 2004 killed pedestrian Carl Snelgrove in a hit and run incident. He had been wearing a tag having been released from prison early on licence.

12

Swift and Certain Sanctions Are an Effective Alternative to Incarceration

National Institute of Justice

The National Institute of Justice is dedicated to improving knowledge and understanding of crime and justice issues through science.

The National Institute of Justice has sponsored the HOPE program (Hawaii's Opportunity Probation with Enforcement), designed to closely observe individuals on probation. The program features "swift and certain sanctions," meaning that individuals who violate probation are brought before a judge quickly and consistently punished. While the program requires more study to determine its effectiveness, early evaluation reveals the program as much more effective than traditional forms of punishment. HOPE has proven helpful in reducing repeat offenders and is generally well-liked by both judges and probation officers.

The HOPE program—Hawaii's Opportunity Probation with Enforcement—is an experimental probation program that emphasizes the delivery of "swift and certain" punishment when a probationer violates conditions of probation.

Positive Effects of Swift and Certain Sanctions

NIJ [National Institute of Justice]-funded researchers evaluated HOPE to determine if it worked and results were positive. Compared to probationers in a control group, after one year the HOPE probationers were:

- Fifty-five percent less likely to be arrested for a new crime.

- Seventy-two percent less likely to use drugs.

- Sixty-one percent less likely to skip appointments with their supervisory officer.

- Fifty-three percent less likely to have their probation revoked.

As a result, HOPE probationers served or were sentenced to 48 percent fewer days, on average, than the control group.

These results were generated using a randomized controlled trial. Researchers used a risk assessment tool to select 493 men and women who had an elevated risk of violating the terms of their probation through drug use, missed appointments or reoffending. Two-thirds of these were randomly assigned to be HOPE probationers and the remainder (the control group) were placed on probation as usual.

The researchers then compared how the two groups were doing at three months, six months, and 12 months.

How HOPE Works

HOPE starts with a formal warning, delivered by a judge in open court, that any violation of probation will result in an immediate, brief jail stay.

Before HOPE, probationers in Hawaii typically received notice of drug tests as much as a month ahead of time. Under HOPE, probationers are given a color code at the warning hearing. Every morning, they must call a hot line to hear which color has been selected for that day. If it is their color, they must appear at the probation office before 2 p.m. for a drug test.

If a HOPE probationer fails to appear for the drug test, a bench warrant is issued and served immediately. A probationer who fails the random drug test is immediately arrested and within 72 hours is brought before a judge. If the probationer is found to have violated the terms of probation, he or she is immediately sentenced to a short jail stay. Typically, the term is several days, servable on the weekend if the probationer is employed; sentences increase for successive violations.

HOPE differs from other programs by:

- Focusing on reducing drug use and missed appointments rather than on drug treatment and imposing drug treatment on every participant.

- Mandating drug treatment for probationers only if they continue to test positive for drug use, or if they request a treatment referral. A HOPE probationer who has a third or fourth missed or "dirty" drug test may be mandated into residential treatment as an alternative to probation revocation.

- Requiring probationers to appear before a judge only when a violation is detected—in this respect, HOPE requires less treatment and court resources than drug courts.

- Having probationers who are employed serve any jail time, at least initially, on a weekend so they do not jeopardize their employment

HOPE Effectively Reduces Probation Violations

The HOPE program is strongly grounded in research that shows that crime generally is committed by people for whom deferred and low-probability threats of severe punishment are less effective than immediate and high-probability threats of mild punishment.

"Swift and certain" punishment for violating terms of probation sends a consistent message to probationers about personal responsibility and accountability. Research has shown that a swift response to an infraction improves the perception that the sanction is fair and that the immediacy is a vital tool in shaping behavior.

Although the HOPE project holds promise, a number of questions can be answered only with more carefully controlled research.

Although the central idea of HOPE is common sense—certainty and swiftness work better than severity—the challenge was how to turn that idea into a reality in the face of scarce resources. Because only a small fraction of HOPE probationers receive mandated treatment, the program can afford to use intensive long-term residential treatment, rather than relying primarily on outpatient drug-free counseling as most diversion programs and drug courts do.

The researchers call this flexible and targeted approach to drug treatment "behavioral triage." They found that HOPE's behavioral triage has several advantages over an assess-and-treat model:

- It is more cost-efficient because it covers a large number of clients while delivering intensive treatment to those who prove to need it.

- It puts a smaller strain on treatment capacity by avoiding the situation in which clients for whom treatment is mandated crowd out clients who voluntarily seek treatment.

- Because the treatment mandate follows repeated failures, it helps break through denial; an offender who has spent three brief spells in jail for dirty drug tests may find it hard to keep telling himself that he is in control of his drug-use.

If treatment is mandated, a HOPE probationer must abstain from drug use (not merely comply with an order to appear for treatment) to avoid a prison term; this, the researchers found, positions the treatment provider as the probationer's ally in the effort to stay in out of jail.

The Impact of HOPE on Courts

In addition to evaluating the effectiveness of HOPE in reducing violations, the researchers also performed a process evaluation. As part of that evaluation, they looked at HOPE's impact on the workloads of probation officers, judges, prosecutors, public defenders and court staff.

The researchers also surveyed general perceptions of HOPE among the probation officers, judges, prosecutors, public defenders and court staff.

Although the central idea of HOPE is common sense, the challenge was how to turn that idea into a reality in the face of scarce resources.

Overall, probation officers, probationers and defense lawyers were enthusiastic about the program. Probation officers had the most favorable view of the program, with nearly 90 percent expressing support for HOPE, followed by judges at 85 percent. Court employees had the most negative general perceptions of HOPE (50 percent); the researchers surmised that this could be due to increased workloads without the countervailing benefit of directly observing improvements in probationer behavior.

Initially, judges gave varying "doses" (the lengths of jail sentences ordered for probation violations), which caused some discontent among probation officers and probationers. But the variation in sentences decreased after the judges learned that research showed no correlation between the length of the jail term and subsequent violation rates.

Additional Research Needed

Although the HOPE project holds promise, a number of questions can be answered only with more carefully controlled research. Such questions include:

- Are the relatively short-term outcomes revealed in the NIJ evaluation—how well the probationers were doing at the one-year mark—sustained for a longer period of time, especially after probationers are released from supervision? NIJ funded a follow-up study that will examine the impact of HOPE among probationers five years after their participation in the program (2004–2006). NIJ expects findings from this study in late 2012.

- Is this approach to offender compliance a cost-effective use of limited resources?

- Which components of the HOPE program are most important; for example, did the drug screening or the punishment schedule—or the interaction of the two—produce the compelling results?

- What types of offenders respond best to the HOPE program?

13

Castration for Sex Offenders Is a Controversial Alternative to Incarceration

Dan Bilefsky

Dan Bilefsky is a reporter for the New York Times.

In Europe, many countries are openly considering laws that allow castration as an option for sex offenders. These laws remain controversial. Many human rights groups consider castration a barbaric punishment. Many law officials in both Europe and the United States, however, suggest that castration can be an effective punishment when traditional punishments fail. Still, the effectiveness of castration remains unknown. While some studies suggest that castration prevents repeat offenses, these studies are not conclusive. Despite factual evidence, lawmakers and even a number of sex offenders support castration as an alternative to traditional punishment.

Pavel remembers the violent night sweats two days before the murder. He went to see a family doctor, who said they would go away. But after viewing a Bruce Lee martial arts film, he said, he felt uncontrollable sexual desires. He invited a 12-year-old neighbor home. Then he stabbed the boy repeatedly.

His psychiatrist says Pavel derived his sexual pleasure from the violence.

More than 20 years have passed. Pavel, then 18, spent seven years in prison and five years in a psychiatric institution. During his last year in prison, he asked to be surgically castrated. Having his testicles removed, he said, was like draining the gasoline from a car hard-wired to crash. A large, dough-faced man, he is sterile and has forsaken marriage, romantic relationships and sex, he said. His life revolves around a Catholic charity, where he is a gardener.

"I can finally live knowing that I am no harm to anybody," he said during an interview at a McDonald's here, as children played loudly nearby. "I am living a productive life. I want to tell people that there is help."

He refused to give his last name for fear of being hounded.

Europeans Debate Castration

Whether castration can help rehabilitate violent sex offenders has come under new scrutiny after the Council of Europe's anti-torture committee last month called surgical castration "invasive, irreversible and mutilating" and demanded that the Czech Republic stop offering the procedure to violent sex offenders. Other critics said that castration threatened to lead society down a dangerous road toward eugenics.

The Czech Republic has allowed at least 94 prisoners over the past decade to be surgically castrated. It is the only country in Europe that uses the procedure for sex offenders. Czech psychiatrists supervising the treatment—a one-hour operation that involves removal of the tissue that produces testosterone—insist that it is the most foolproof way to tame sexual urges in dangerous predators suffering from extreme sexual disorders.

Surgical castration has been a means of social control for centuries. In ancient China, eunuchs were trusted to serve the imperial family inside the palace grounds; in Italy several centuries ago, youthful male choir members were castrated to preserve their high singing voices.

These days it can be used to treat testicular cancer and some advanced cases of prostate cancer.

Now, more countries in Europe are considering requiring or allowing chemical castration for violent sex offenders. There is intense debate over whose rights take precedence: those of sex offenders, who could be subjected to a punishment that many consider cruel, or those of society, which expects protection from sexual predators.

Poland is expected to become the first nation of the European Union to give judges the right to impose chemical castration on at least some convicted pedophiles, using hormonal drugs to curb sexual appetite; the impetus for the change was the arrest of a 45-year-old man in September who had fathered two children by his young daughter. Spain, after a convicted pedophile killed a child, is considering plans to offer chemical castration.

Castration Versus Incarceration

Last year, the governor of Louisiana, Bobby Jindal, signed legislation requiring courts to order chemical castration for offenders convicted of certain sex crimes a second time.

In the Czech Republic, the issue was brought home last month when Antonin Novak, 43, was sentenced to life in prison after raping and killing Jakub Simanek, a 9-year-old boy who disappeared last May. Mr. Novak, who had served four and a half years in prison for sexual offenses in Slovakia, had been ordered to undergo outpatient treatment, but had failed to show up several months before the murder. Advocates of surgical castration argued that had he been castrated, the tragedy could have been prevented.

Hynek Blasko, Jakub's father, expressed indignation that human rights groups were putting the rights of criminals ahead of those of victims. "My personal tragedy is that my son is in heaven and he is never coming back, and all I have left of him is 1.5 kilograms of ashes," he said in an interview.

"No one wants to touch the rights of the pedophiles, but what about the rights of a 9-year-old boy with his life ahead of him?"

Ales Butala, a Slovenian human rights lawyer who led the Council of Europe's delegation to the Czech Republic, argued that surgical castration was unethical, because it was not medically necessary and deprived castrated men of the right to reproduce. He also challenged its effectiveness, saying that the council's committee had discovered three cases of castrated Czech sex offenders who had gone on to commit violent crimes, including pedophilia and attempted murder.

Although the procedure is voluntary, Mr. Butala said that he believed some offenders felt they had no choice.

"Sex offenders are requesting castration in hope of getting released from a life of incarceration," he said. "Is that really free and informed consent?"

But government health officials here and some Czech psychiatrists counter that castration can be effective and argue that by seeking to outlaw the practice, the council is putting potential victims at risk.

A Danish study of 900 castrated sex offenders in the 1960s suggested the rate of repeat offences dropped after surgical castration to 2.3 percent from 80 percent.

Reducing Repeat Offenders

Dr. Martin Holly, a leading sexologist and psychiatrist who is director of the Psychiatric Hospital Bohnice in Prague, said none of the nearly 100 sex offenders who had been physically castrated had committed further offenses.

A Danish study of 900 castrated sex offenders in the 1960s suggested the rate of repeat offenses dropped after surgical castration to 2.3 percent from 80 percent.

But human rights groups say that such studies are inconclusive because they rely on self-reporting by sex offenders. Other psychiatric experts argue that sexual pathology is in the brain and cannot be cured by surgery.

Dr. Holly, who has counseled convicted sex offenders for four decades, stressed that the procedure was being allowed only for repeat violent offenders who suffered from severe sexual disorders. Moreover, he said, the procedure is undertaken only with the informed consent of the patient and with the approval of an independent committee of psychiatric and legal experts.

Several states, including Texas, Florida, and California, now allow or mandate chemical castration for certain convicted sex offences.

Jaroslav Novak, chief of urology at the Faculty Hospital Na Bulovce in Prague, said: "This is not a very common procedure. We carry it out maybe once every one to two years at most."

Several states, including Texas, Florida, and California, now allow or mandate chemical castration for certain convicted sex offenders.

Dr. Fred S. Berlin, founder of the Sexual Disorders Clinic at Johns Hopkins University, argued that chemical castration was less physically harmful than surgery and that it provided a safeguard, because a psychiatrist could inform the courts or police if the patient ordered to undergo treatment failed to show up. A surgically castrated patient, Dr. Berlin said, can order testosterone over the Internet.

For Hynek Blasko, the father of Jakub Simanek, neither form of castration is the answer. "These people must be under permanent detention where they can be monitored," he said. "There has to be a difference between the rights of the victim and the perpetrator."

14

Reading Courses Offer an Effective Alternative to Incarceration

Anna Barker

Anna Barker is a contributor to the Guardian.

While Texas is known for its no-nonsense approach to crime, it is also the home of Changing Lives Through Literature (CLTL). With the CLTL program, convicted individuals are sentenced to reading groups instead of traditional punishments. Within the reading groups, men and women (in gender separated groups) discuss literary classics like John Steinbeck's novel Of Mice and Men. *Because of the success of the program, other localities have imported versions of it. In England there is a version of the program called Stories Connect, and while it has shown success, it has not yet been supported by the criminal justice system. Although literature programs are considered soft on crime by detractors, supporters believe that these programs can change lives.*

With one of the highest incarceration rates in the world, and the death penalty, the US state of Texas seems the last place to embrace a liberal-minded alternative to prison. But when Mitchell Rouse was convicted of two drug offences in Houston, the former x-ray technician who faced a 60-year prison sentence—reduced to 30 years if he pleaded guilty—was instead put on probation and sentenced to read.

"I was doing it because it was a condition of my probation and it would reduce my community hours," Rouse recalls.

The 42-year-old had turned to drugs as a way of coping with the stress of his job at a hospital where he frequently worked an 80-hour week. But cooking up to a gram of crystal meth a day to feed his habit gradually took its toll on his life at home, which he shared with his wife and three young children. Finally, fearing for his life, Mitchell's wife turned him into the authorities. "If she hadn't, I would be dead or destitute by now," he says.

Five years on, he is free from drugs, holding down a job as a building contractor, and reunited with his family. He describes being sentenced to a reading group as "a miracle" and says the six-week reading course "changed the way I look at life".

"It made me believe in my own potential. In the group you're not wrong, you're not necessarily right either, but your opinion is just as valid as anyone else's," he says.

Changing Lives Through Literature

Rouse is one of thousands of offenders across the US who, as an alternative to prison, are placed on a rehabilitation programme called Changing Lives Through Literature (CLTL). Repeat offenders of serious crimes such as armed robbery, assault or drug dealing are made to attend a reading group where they discuss literary classics such as *To Kill a Mockingbird* [by Harper Lee], *The Bell Jar* [by Sylvia Plath] and *Of Mice and Men* [by John Steinbeck].

Rouse's group was run by part-time lecturer in liberal studies at Rice University in Houston, Larry Jablecki, who uses the texts of Plato, Mill and Socrates to explore themes of fate, love, anger, liberty, tolerance and empathy. "I particularly liked some of the ideas in John Stuart Mill's *On Liberty*," says Mitchell, who now wants to do a PhD in philosophy.

Groups are single sex and the books chosen resonate with some of the issues the offenders may be facing. A male group, for example, may read books with a theme of male identity. A judge, a probation officer and an academic join a session of 30 offenders to talk about issues as equals.

Of the 597 who have completed the course in Brazoria County, Texas, between 1997 and 2008, only 36 (6%) had their probations revoked and were sent to jail.

A year-long study of the first cohort that went through the programme, which was founded in Massachusetts in 1991, found that only 19% had reoffended compared with 42% in a control group. And those from the programme who did reoffend committed less serious crimes.

CLTL is the brainchild of Robert Waxler, a professor of English at University of Massachusetts Dartmouth. As an experiment, he convinced his friend, Judge Kane, to take eight criminals who repeatedly came before him and place them on a reading programme that Waxler had devised instead of sending them to prison. It now runs in eight states including Texas, Arizona and New York.

The public have been largely won over by the success rates and how cheap the programme is to run.

Reading Reform in England

In the UK, nearly half of prisoners reoffend within a year of being released from jail. Could programmes like CLTL work on this side of the Atlantic where Ken Clarke, in his first major speech as justice secretary, indicated that more offenders could be given community sentences by putting a greater emphasis on what he terms "intelligent sentencing"?

Lady Stern, senior research fellow at the international centre for prison studies at King's College London, is not convinced. "Research does show that the public are largely pro-rehabilitation, but when you take an idea that involves offenders attending a university campus to be part of a reading group, instead of being sentenced to prison, it asks a lot of even the most thoughtful and socially conscious public," she says.

The initiative was initially met with an inevitable flurry of criticism in the US. Waxler and his supporters were described as "bleeding-heart liberals".

"They were shocked at the idea of offenders going on to university campuses to read books for free while the students were paying their way through education," says Waxler. "Some even thought the offenders would steal from them. It only takes one person to prove them right, but it's never happened."

In Texas, the public have been largely won over by the success rates and how cheap the programme is to run. Instead of spending a lifetime in prison at a cost of more than $30,000 (£19,520) a year, Rouse's "rehabilitation" cost the taxpayer just $500 (£325). But it is the experiences of offenders, some of whom have never read a book before, that Waxler points to.

"In one group we read *The Old Man and the Sea* by Ernest Hemingway," he recalls. "The story focuses on Santiago, an old fisherman in Cuba, and opens with some heartache: Santiago is not able to catch fish. We talk about him and the endurance he seems to represent, the very fact that he gets up every morning despite the battering he takes.

"The following time the group meet, one of the offenders wants to share something. He'd been walking down Main Street and he said he could hear, metaphorically speaking, the voices of his neighbourhood. He'd been thinking about returning to his old life, to drugs, but as he listened to those voices, he also heard the voice of Santiago. If Santiago could continue to get up each day and make the right choice then he could do too."

Santiago, a character in a novel, had become the offender's role model. For many offenders, some of whom have spent half their lives in jail, it is the first time they've had a worthy model, says Waxler.

Literacy is a problem. Offenders are unlikely to be sentenced to the programme if they cannot read. However, those with poor reading are not excluded. The groups may read short stories, or excerpts from a novel may be read aloud so that low-level readers can participate.

Changing Lives in the UK

In the UK, a version of the programme called Stories Connect is running in a handful of prisons with some success, and in Exeter it has recently moved out into the community for people with drug and alcohol problems. But it does not yet have the support of the criminal justice system, so cannot be an alternative sentencing option for the courts.

Retired probation officer Louise Ross voluntarily runs the small group in Exeter. Participants are referred from the Exeter and North Devon Addiction Service, and were, until three-year funding from the Paul Hamlyn Foundation ran out in April, made to attend as part of a community service order. Now all attendance is voluntary, but stories of how the programme changes lives are no less impressive.

After years of opiate abuse, Steve Rowe, 50, who joined the first Exeter group three years ago, says: "Stories Connect didn't just change my life, it saved it." He explains: "We looked at a section of *Oliver Twist*, the relationship between Bill Sikes and Nancy. One of us pretended we were Bill while everyone else asked questions. The idea was you responded as much as you could from that character's point of view. It makes you think about what others think and feel, and really helps you to reflect on yourself."

Mary Stephenson, a writer, who runs Stories Connect, says more funding is needed. To date, in Exeter, 96 people have been through the programme, but of these only 29 completed the course. This, she says, is largely due to the chaotic lives of the participants, many of whom are battling with drug problems, and the fact that the groups are not an alternative to prison, which removes the main incentive.

There are plans, again subject to funding, for the University of Exeter to run a research project into the effectiveness of the programme in the UK, both inside prisons and out. But until then, there are no quantitative results that prove the programme reduces reoffending.

Next week, Stephenson is attending a roundtable meeting with prisons and probation minister Crispin Blunt, at which she will make the point that the programme could be achieving so much more.

"In terms of tackling reoffending, we need both more funding and the political support to explore it," says Stephenson. "There's no doubt among the people I've worked with that the success in America could be repeated here."

Waxler agrees: "I think that one of the great testaments of this programme is that it demonstrates clearly that literature can make a difference to people's lives," he says. "I already believed that, but I knew it could also be used to rehabilitate offenders."

Rouse says it is hard to judge how much the reading group should take credit for turning his life around as he'd already made the decision to change.

"I didn't want to lose my family," he says. "But the group did give me the guidance and direction I needed in my life, and without it I'd have spent the rest of my life in jail. It gave me a second chance."

Organizations to Contact

The editors have compiled the following list of organizations concerned with the issues debated in this book. The descriptions are derived from materials provided by the organizations. All have publications or information available for interested readers. The list was compiled on the date of publication of the present volume; names, addresses, phone and fax numbers, and e-mail and Internet addresses may change. Be aware that many organizations take several weeks or longer to respond to inquiries, so allow as much time as possible.

American Civil Liberties Union (ACLU)
National Prison Project, Washington, DC   20005
(202) 549-2666
e-mail: aclu@aclu.org
website: www.aclu.org

Formed in 1972, the ACLU's National Prison Project is a re-source center that works to protect the rights of adult and juvenile offenders. It opposes electronic monitoring of offenders and the privatization of prisons. The project publishes the quarterly *National Prison Project Journal* and various booklets.

American Correctional Association (ACA)
206 N. Washington Street, Suite 200, Alexandria, VA   22314
(800) 222-5646
website: www.aca.org

ACA is committed to improving national and international correctional policy and to promoting the professional development of those working in the field of corrections. It offers a variety of books and courses on the criminal justice system. ACA publishes the bimonthly magazine *Corrections Today*.

American Jail Association (AJA)

1135 Professional Court, Hagerstown, MD   21740-5853

(301) 790-3930

website: www.aja.org

Formed in 1981, the AJA is a national, nonprofit organization dedicated to supporting those who work in and operate the nation's jails. It publishes *American Jails* magazine.

Center for Alternative Sentencing and Employment Services (CASES)

346 Broadway, 3rd Floor, New York, NY   10013

(212) 732-0076 • fax: (212) 571-0292

e-mail: info@cases.org

website: www.cases.org

CASES seeks to end what it views as the overuse of incarceration as a response to crime. It operates two alternative-sentencing programs in New York City: the Court Employment Project, which provides intensive supervision and services for felony offenders, and the Community Service Sentencing Project, which works with repeat misdemeanor offenders. The center advocates in court for offenders' admission into its programs. CASES publishes various program brochures.

Citizens Alliance on Prisons and Public Spending (CAPPS)

403 Seymour Ave., Suite 200, Lansing, MI   48933

(517) 482-7753 • fax: (517) 482-7754

e-mail: capps@capps-mi.org

website: www.capps-mi.org

CAPPS is a nonprofit public policy organization concerned about the social and economic costs of prison expansion. It opposes the incarceration of criminals that pose no risk to society. Its website contains extensive information about how and why prison populations should be reduced, plus profiles of specific prisoners that it believes should be paroled.

Critical Resistance

1904 Franklin St., Suite 504, Oakland, CA   94612
(510) 444-0484 • fax: (510) 444-2177
e-mail: crnational@criticalresistance.org
website: www.criticalresistance.org

Critical Resistance is an activist group opposed to incarcerating people in prisons, maintaining that prison is not an effective response to poverty and crime. The group advocates the immediate release of all nonviolent offenders from the US prison system. It publishes several reports offering alternatives to incarceration on its website, including "A Plan to Save the State of California a Billion Dollars."

Families Against Mandatory Minimums (FAMM)

1612 K St. NW, Suite 700, Washington, DC   20006
(202) 822-6700 • fax: (202) 822-6704
e-mail: famm@famm.org
website: www.famm.org

FAMM is an educational organization that works to repeal mandatory minimum sentences. It provides legislators, the public, and the media with information on, and analyses of, mandatory-sentencing laws. FAMM publishes the quarterly newsletter *FAMMGram*.

Justice Policy Institute

1012 14th St. NW, Suite 400, Washington, DC   20005
(202) 558-7974 • (202) 558-7978
e-mail: info@justicepolicy.org
website: www.justicepolicy.org

The Justice Policy Institute is a nonprofit research and public policy organization dedicated to ending society's reliance on incarceration and promoting just and effective solutions to America's social problems. The Justice Policy Institute has published numerous reports and articles debating crime and punishment in America, including *Poor Prescription: The Cost of Imprisoning Drug Offenders in the United States* and *The Punishing Decade*.

National Center on Institutions and Alternatives (NCIA)
7222 Ambassador Rd., Baltimore, MD   21244
(443) 780-1300 • fax: (401) 597-9656
website: www.ncianet.org

NCIA is a criminal justice foundation that supports community-based alternatives to prison, contending that they are more effective at providing the education, training, and personal skills required for the rehabilitation of nonviolent offenders. The center advocates doubling "good conduct" credit for the early release of nonviolent first-time offenders in the federal prison system to make room for violent offenders. NCIA publishes books, reports, and the periodic newsletters *Criminal Defense Update* and *Jail Suicide/Mental Health Update*.

The Sentencing Project
1705 DeSales Street NW, 8th Floor, Washington, DC   20036
(202) 628-0871 • fax: (202) 628-1091
e-mail: staff@sentencingproject.org
website: www.sentencingproject.org

The Sentencing Project seeks to provide public defenders and other public officials with information on establishing and improving alternative sentencing programs that provide convicted persons with positive and constructive options to incarceration. It promotes increased public understanding of the sentencing process and alternative sentencing programs. The Sentencing Project publishes many reports on US prisons including *Facts About Prison and Prisoners* and *Prison Privatization and the Use of Incarceration*.

Urban Institute (UI)
2100 M St. NW, Washington, DC   20037
(202) 833-7200
e-mail: paffairs@ui.urban.org
website: www.urban.org

UI is a nonpartisan research organization that conducts regular studies on a wide array of social issues. Its research on America's prison system maintains that inmates are not receiving enough rehabilitative programming or adequate life-skills preparation prior to release. Its reports on prison reform, posted on UI's website, include *A Portrait of Prisoner Reentry in Illinois* and *Parole in California, 1980–2000: Implications for Reform.*

Bibliography

Books

Michael Alexander	*The New Jim Crow: Mass Incarceration in the Age of Colorblindness.* New York: New Press, 2010.
Michelle Brown	*The Culture of Punishment: Prison, Society, and Spectacle.* New York: New York University, 2009.
K.C. Carceral	*Prison, Inc.: A Convict Exposes Life Inside a Private Prison.* New York: New York University, 2005.
David Cayley	*Expanding Prisons: The Crisis of Crime and Punishment and the Search for Alternatives.* Toronto, Ontario: House of Anansi, 1998.
Angela Y. Davis	*Are Prisons Obsolete?* New York: Seven Stories, 2003.
Erin George	*A Woman Doing Life: Notes from a Prison for Women.* New York: Oxford University, 2010.
Robert Ellis Gordon	*The Funhouse Mirror: Reflections on Prison.* Pullman, WA: Washington State University, 2000.
Stephen John Hartnett, ed.	*Challenging the Prison-Industrial Complex: Activism, Arts, and Educational Alternatives.* Champaign, IL: University of Illinois, 2011.

Tara Herival and Paul Wright, eds.	*Prison Profiteers: Who Makes Money from Mass Incarceration.* New York: New Press, 2009.
T.J. Parsell	*Fish: A Memoir of a Boy in a Man's Prison.* New York: Da Capo, 2007.
Jeffery Ian Ross and Stephen C. Richards	*Behind Bars: Surviving Prison.* New York: Alpha, 2002.
Michael G. Santos	*Inside: Life Behind Bars in America.* New York: St. Martin's Griffin, 2007.
William Upski Wimsatt	*No More Prisons.* New York: Soft Skull, 2008.

Periodicals

Arkansas Business	"Prison Alternatives," July 28, 2003.
Atlantic.com	"Is America's Incarceration Rate a Labor Market Outcome?" June 1, 2009.
Chesa Boudin	"Children Left Behind," *The Nation*, September 29, 2003.
Current Events, a Weekly Reader Publication	"Shame, Shame, Shame!" October 29, 2007.
Economist	"If Not Jail, What?" December 5, 1995.
Kai Falkenberg	"How Business Crooks Cut Their Jail Time," *Forbes*, January 12, 2009.

David C. Fathi — "The Challenge of Prison Oversight," *American Criminal Law Review*, Fall 2010.

Earl Ofari Hutchinson — "Jena 6 Case Highlights Injustice: Louisiana Investigation Found a Juvenile Justice System in Trouble," *National Catholic Reporter*, October 5, 2007.

Patrick Hyde — "Day Reporting Eases Jail Overcrowding," *American City & County*, September 1, 2006.

Illinois Bar Journal — "Illinois Redeploy Program Amended," June 2009.

Dahlia Lithwick — "Our Real Prison Problem," *Newsweek*, June 15, 2009.

Sara Maitland — "Our Love Affair with Low Life," *New Statesman*, September 2000.

Stephanie Mencimer — "Righting Sentences: Let's Get Smart About Who Should—And Shouldn't—Be in Jail," *Washington Monthly*, April 1993.

Teresa Mitchell — "Creative Sentencing," *LawNow*, July–August 2008.

James Sterngold — "Worst of the Worst: Californias Hard Lessons in How Not to Run a Prison System," *Mother Jones*, July–August 2008.

Steve Varnam — "Our Prisons Are a Crime," *Christianity Today*, June 21, 1993.

Claire Walker   "Young Offenders Deserve a
                     Hearing," *New Statesman*, April 17,
                     2000.

Kurt Williamsen   "Judges Getting Creative: Much to
                     the Dismay of Some Liberal Activists,
                     More and More Judges Are Devising
                     Creative Punishments for Criminals
                     as Alternatives to Sentences which
                     Send Violators to Prison," *New
                     American*, December 27, 2004.

Robert Worth   "Making Criminals Pay," *Washington
                     Monthly*, December 1998.

Index